THE SONG OF MOSES

The Song of Moses

A Theological Quarry

GEORGE A. F. KNIGHT

WILLIAM B. EERDMANS PUBLISHING COMPANY
GRAND RAPIDS, MICHIGAN

Copyright © 1995 by Wm. B. Eerdmans Publishing Co.

255 Jefferson Ave. S.E., Grand Rapids, Michigan 49503

Printed in the United States of America

00 99 98 97 96 95   7 6 5 4 3 2 1

Library of Congress Cataloging-in-Publication Data

Knight, George Angus Fulton, 1909-

The song of Moses: a theological quarry / George A. F. Knight.

p.   cm.

Includes bibliographical references.

ISBN 0-8028-0599-X (pbk.)

1. Bible. O. T. Deuteronomy XXXII, 1-43 — Commentaries.

I. Title.

BS1275.3.K56 1994

222′.15077 — dc20   94-23343

CIP

Contents

v

Abbreviations

Bab.	Babylonian Talmud
KJV	King James Version
LXX	Septuagint
MT	Masoretic Text
NEB	New English Bible
NJB	New Jerusalem Bible
NJV	New Jewish Version
NRSV	New Revised Standard Version
NT	New Testament
OT	Old Testament
REV	Revised English Bible
RSV	Revised Standard Version
TEV	Today's English Version

Preface

This volume is a commentary on the so-called Song of Moses, which comprises forty-three verses of chapter 32 of Deuteronomy. Though not part of the International Theological Commentary series, this commentary is in full accord with its aims: to offer a theological interpretation of the Hebrew text; to include perspectives not limited to the thoughts and lifestyles of the "Christian" West, reading the Hebrew Scriptures in the twin contexts of ancient Israel and our modern day; and to proclaim the biblical message as the revelation of God which, when rightly received, brings *shalom* to both the individual and the community.

As a commentary, this book is addressed to ministers, priests, and Christian educators who seek to move beyond the commonly used "historical critical" approach to the Bible and to take the next step. Since the Old Testament is the book of the believing community, both Jewish and Christian, its text has acquired ever more meaning through an ongoing interpretation. This growth of interpretation may be found within the Bible itself and in the continuing scholarship of the Synagogue and the Church.

Verse-by-verse comments are made from the New Revised Standard Version (NRSV), which has been hailed as undoubtedly the ecumenical version in the English language for the coming century.

Dunedin N. Z.   GEORGE A. F. KNIGHT

Introduction

For many years scholars took it for granted that the Song of Moses was composed, in the spirit of Moses, probably in the seventh century B.C.E., when the rest of the book of Deuteronomy found its present form. This was when the two kings Manasseh and Amon reigned in Jerusalem, both of whose reigns are summed up in the words of 2 Kings — "he did what was evil in the sight of the Lord." We have no record of any prophetic figure being able to make himself heard in that half-century. What happened was, to use a modern phrase, "true religion went underground."

It was in that forty- to fifty-year period, scholarly opinion suggests, that "prophecy" was compelled to take the form of writing. It seems that ancient written material, going right back to Moses, having been carefully preserved in both kingdoms, was now quietly collated, supplemented, brought up to date, and applied to the very changed and developed life of Israel. This was now an Israel living centuries later than the wilderness conditions under which Moses had lived, Moses who had never known the Promised Land. These unknown editors of Deuteronomy, we believe, entered upon their task in the faith that the Mosaic material was indeed the Word of God. Consequently it was "alive" even as the living God is alive. This is evident when we note how Moses in Deuteronomy is figured as speaking "to

1

this day." This is what thoughtful young king Josiah, who came to the throne in 640 B.C.E., also believed of it when in his day a book or scroll was discovered in the temple in a cupboard that was meant for holding the accoutrements of worship (2 Kgs. 23:1-3).

Looking back from their period in history, the editors suggest that Moses foresaw how, after his death, "this people will begin to prostitute themselves to the foreign gods in their midst. . . . They will forsake me, breaking my covenant that I have made with them" (Deut. 31:16, a passage which is placed as an introduction to the Song found in ch. 32). Their sin would be twofold. (1) They would apostatize and so break the First Commandment; and (2) they would break the bond of *hesed* which bound Yahweh to them. God's hope and plan was that they would maintain "steadfast love" toward himself, as the RSV translates this key theological term throughout the Old Testament, even as God consistently maintained that kind of love toward Israel (cf. Ps. 136). Yahweh's wrath, therefore, would have to be kindled against them "in that day," and Yahweh would necessarily "hide his face" from them (Deut. 31:17). Chapter 31 goes on to declare that the LORD actually "induced" Moses (as Gerhard von Rad expresses it) to write down the Song that follows, that it "will confront them as a witness" (31:21). Then he was to speak it out "in their hearing." Consequently we also are to read the Song now as a witness for God, and as God's own "answer" (von Rad) addressed to us.

Since 32:45-47 are in the form of a commandment commending the "Law" (the Torah) to Israel, with reference back to 31:24, the Song has been seen as a "living" interpretation of the Torah — that is, as much of it as Moses was able to leave in Israel's care at his death. What the Deuteronomists have succeeded in doing is to show that the Torah is not merely a collection of words, words, words, but is in fact the veritable Word of God, for it is no less than "your very life" (32:47).

Interestingly therefore, the Deuteronomists conjoin the call to "life" with the death of Moses in the very next verse. This

2

leaves us of course with a theological challenge. Moses was a sinner just as were all his people, as we read at 32:51. Although the wages of sin is death (Exod. 32:30-34), yet Moses dies in peace and, according to the Hebrew text, God "buries" him (Deut. 34:6).

In parallel with the "updating" of Moses' work, which until recently had been accepted by scholars, went the updating of Moses' theological understanding of Israel's covenant relationship with Yahweh, as expressed in the Song. In fact, C. H. Cornill describes the poem as "a compendium of the prophetic theology" (*Introduction to the Canonical Books of the OT,* 123). Until comparatively recently critical study sought to separate what was thought to be the original text of the Song from later accretions over the period from Moses' death until the time of Josiah, with the presupposition that the Song embodied an understanding of God that developed through the period of the Monarchy even up to the first Isaiah. In that spirit scholars (as recently as William F. Albright, Patrick W. Skehan, Frank M. Cross, Harold L. Ginsberg, N. H. Tur-Sinai) regularly made many emendations to its text to fit it into this prevailing view.

New light was thrown upon the Song with the discovery at Ras Shamra in 1928 of literary material written in Ugaritic, a language closely related to Biblical Hebrew. It was recognized at once when it was deciphered by 1931-32 that here was material contemporary with the life of Moses. Accordingly some of what had been regarded as impossible to impute to Moses was acknowledged as quite possibly belonging to his period. William F. Albright in the United States was one who courageously changed his mind. He had come to the conclusion that the date of Israel's exodus from Egypt could be fixed at about 1290, so that the entry into Canaan would then be around 1250. If this were so, then the date would be roughly that of the Song. That is, it would originate some 250 years before the accession of David to the throne, an event usually suggested to be about 1000. Almost simultaneously, moreover, Otto Eissfeldt in Germany reached much the same series of dates, and they were then followed by a number of scholars. This dating of the Song was thus revolutionary.

This dating was instigated by research on the very early poems that have survived in the Pentateuch, such as Exod. 15:1-12, the Song of the Sea, sung after the escape from Egypt (vv. 13-18 seem to be a later addition from the period after the Settlement — perhaps even from David's time); Exod. 15:21, the Song of Miriam; Deut. 33, the Blessing of Moses; the poems in the book of Numbers; the Song of Deborah, Judg. 5:2-31; and others. There is no doubt left now of their pre-Davidic origin.

It was noted that the style of the Song of Moses was intermediate between the archaic repetitive parallelism of the Songs of Miriam (Exod 15:21, only two lines!) and Deborah (Judg. 5), for example, and of the poems of the classical period, such as the Lament of David, 2 Sam. 22. But there is no point in the older modern idea of dividing the Song of Moses into stanzas. The poem is one whole, divisible only by the ebb and flow of Moses' vision and mood (Roland de Vaux).

In parallel with these linguistic studies, however, there has been a growing awareness that in the pre-Davidic period (i.e., in the pre-literate period, when only a small elite could ever write, as Moses learned to do in Egypt) men's and women's ability to learn by heart — to memorize even long epic poems and tribal myths and legends — was much greater than we have been predisposed to recognize in our day of the endless publication of written matter. It has been my privilege to teach students from a dozen or more cultures at one time, none of whom possessed a literary heritage, but they had highly trained memories. This enabled them both to pick up strange languages in a matter of weeks, and to be able to recount exactly the myths of their tribal heritage. The Maori people of New Zealand, for example, had never possessed a written language until the coming of the Europeans less than two hundred years ago. Yet I meet Maori youth today who can recite with total accuracy their genealogical tree stemming from about A.D. 1400 or even earlier.

4

Charles Nicholl writes in *Borderlines: A Journey in Thailand and Burma* (New York: Viking, 1988): "Like many tribal peoples, the *Akha* people in the 'Golden Triangle,' so-called, find that their sense of tradition is expressed as a revering of 'ancestors.' Some *Akha* are said to be able to recite a genealogy of fifty or sixty names, beginning with their own forebears, and going back through the clan chiefs, real and legendary, to the 'great father' of the *Akha* race, Zoeh Tah Pah" (142).

But more, as we learn from such Pacific peoples as the Samoans, the Cook Islanders, and the Tongans, details of their histories were passed down by action songs from parents to children. Similarly, it seems, the strong traditions of the early Israelites were preserved in poetry and mime until the time came to celebrate the ascent to the throne of a new king. This was done by active dramatization of what had led up to that moment, as a theological justification for the choice of king was taught to the people.

Consequently, early Hebrew literary sources are to be clarified, not so much from archaeological research as from the poetic tradition of the Arabian peninsula. The first enemy the Hebrews encountered in the Sinai peninsula was the Amalekites (Exod. 17:8). This group was really only a branch of the desert Arabs of the area. They would thus be inheritors of the Arabian ability to learn and then to recite great numbers of interconnected poems, by means of which they passed on to the rising generation the stories of the mighty deeds of their ancestors.

As Clement Huart puts it in *A History of Arabic Literature:* "The *hida* was the song of the leading camel-driver of the caravan. It was evidently unconsciously invented by the native genius of the Bedouin for poetic rhythm. . . . In this way tribal memories were stirred and transmitted down the centuries" (5, 10) Just as the Song of Moses has survived, so have the most ancient pre-Islamic poems which form the collection of the seven *mu'allaqat*, though these of course bear a name given to them at a much later date.

In all probability, then, professional holy men in the period of the judges would "perform" at social gatherings, some of which might have been held around a well on a summer evening. In this way the stories of the Patriarchs and of the days in the wilderness would be passed down the generations, as was regarded as vital by Moses himself (Deut. 32:7).

From the end of Moses' life until the growth of education and of written records in the mid-900s is a span of only about three hundred years, a period easily covered if Moses' command was adhered to. Moreover, his teaching was expressed not in mere prose, but in much more easily memorized verse. What is more, it was not just recited, it was sung (thus the *song* of Moses) when father attempted to teach son, by getting the boy to sing back to him what he had learned until the son was finally word perfect.

The summation of all this is that we need no longer suppose that the Song of Moses was composed in that "underground movement" which preceded King Josiah's reign and the life of the prophet Jeremiah. Rather, we can be assured now that the Song does truly originate from Moses, was repeated orally for a couple of centuries, and was then given fixed form in the proto-Hebraic script which Solomon's schools taught their young students to acquire. Anyway, as Martin Noth points out, "The basic tradition in the Pentateuch is oral."

Solomon's marriage to an Egyptian princess about 960 (1 Kgs. 3:1) opened up for the Israelites the vast experience of Egypt in learning and government. This event coincided with the period when Moses' Song probably found its written form. It is interesting therefore to note that there is not a trace of the Egyptian philosophy of life in the Song such as might have been written into it by the wisdom teachers at the royal court.

Also note that one should assign "the theologumenon expressed in Deut. 32:8-9 to the older, premonarchic material" (J. J. M. Roberts, "The Davidic Origin of the Zion Tradition," 340, n. 71); and note also that Moses' acquaintance with the Ugaritic corpus could be easily attributed to his friendship with his educated father-in-law, Jethro.

Theologically speaking, the first song of Moses, recorded at Exod. 15:1-12, sets the tone for the whole of the Mosaic literature. It is not about religion, nor is it about Israel. Far less is it about Moses himself. It is about God: "I will sing to the LORD, for *he* has triumphed gloriously . . . *he* has become my salvation." It is not even about the Torah; no reference is made to the Decalogue. Deut. 32, however, emphasizes the basic importance of the First Commandment. Again, if Moses' poem had been a seventh-sixth-century work, there would surely have been a reference to the keeping of the sabbath, for that was an issue which had become central by the time of Jeremiah.

As for Moses himself, here we have a uniquely important servant of God. (1) He was the one who led an undiscipled rabble of slaves out of their Egyptian servitude. (2) He was the one who received Yahweh's revelation of himself to the people, and so to the world. (3) He was the mediator of the Covenant between Yahweh and his people, along with the essential elements of the Torah. Note, therefore, that Moses did not "found" a religion in the sense of establishing its institutions and its teaching. "What he did is nothing compared with what God did. . . . Moses . . . was at the beginning of this movement that only in the course of a long process of development became a world religion" (Roland de Vaux, *The Early History of Israel,* 453-54). That is why Jesus did not "found" a religion either. He "found" one that was already there.

Here is a reality of which few in this generation are aware. This is essentially because few theological students are advised or encouraged to study Hebrew, their teachers assuming that a knowledge of Greek alone, leading to a study of the New Testament and of the Greek Septuagint, is all that is needed for a grasp of biblical theology. "Westcott's real attitude to 'theological' systems is indicated in one most significant sentence in his essay on Origen: 'No fact, I think, is sadder in the history of religious thought than that Augustine had no real knowledge of Greek'" (W. Robertson Nicoll, *Princes of the Church,* 145). One should add that he had no knowledge of Hebrew at all. In fact, many of the present-day "deviations" depend on Augustine for their theology. For example, a foremost "evangelical" writer has published a whole volume on "Love in the Bible" without ever mentioning the Old Testament. Likewise, a leading Pentecostalist recently gave a public lecture on the significance of the Holy Spirit, but paid no attention to that part of the Bible which St. Paul called "The Scriptures." At long last, however, the study of Hebrew is being made mandatory in some of the best theological schools, so that a much more scholarly approach may be made to the study both of Christology and of the doctrine of the Holy Trinity.

Commentary

v. 1   Give ear, O heavens, and I will speak;
     let the earth hear the words of my mouth.

At once we are faced with the issue as to who is speaking here. Who is saying, "I will speak"? Who refers to "the words of my mouth" and in v. 2 to "my teaching"? The answer is not a simple one, such as "Of course, it is Moses who is speaking; the Deuteronomist has told us so" (31:30). We note that none of the later prophets believed that they spoke merely the ideas that their own mind had produced. For example, Hosea's editor begins his book with the phrase "The word of the LORD that 'came to' (*hayah el*) Hosea" (Hos. 1:1). Again in Jonah 1:1 we have, "Now the word of the LORD 'came to' Jonah." Although the Song of Moses is not headed in this manner, surely the "Word" "came" to Moses also, for Moses was later regarded as the exemplar of all biblical prophets (cf. Deut. 18:15; Luke 16:31). He is speaking at this juncture right at the end of his long life. As Deut. 31:28 informs us, Moses quite humbly asks if he may "recite these words," as if he were well aware of his own frailty, and that the inspiration behind them was not his own.

A point we should keep in mind is that in the case of some of our oldest OT material no distinction is made between the speech of God and the speech of his messenger (e.g., Gen.

18:1-14, especially v. 13); or again, incorporated into the Covenant Code we hear God actually "ordaining" his messenger (mal'ak) to speak and act as if the messenger himself were God (Exod. 23:20-21). It is no surprise, then, to find at v. 3 of our Song that Moses "says" what God has already proclaimed to him at Sinai about himself (Exod. 34:5-7). It is naive of those scholars who suggest that such a self-description of God's nature as we meet with there could have been penned only in later centuries. We may well ask why "later centuries" should know more about God than Moses who had lived through the escape from Egypt.

Moses apostrophizes nature. So do many prophets and psalmists like Moses in years to come. First, the skies are to "give ear." "Let me speak," he says. "I propose to say something" — evidently something of great import. A high theme demands a supreme audience. Then, second, the earth must listen to "the *words* of my mouth." We note this unusual noun, for *imrey* occurs in poetry only in the OT, with but one exception. Speech is not mere sound. It is a vital, active, and creative entity in itself, in that it has emerged first from the "heart" and then from the lips of a human mouth. A word spoken "with intent" — that is, anything other than idle chatter — is effective; it reaches its objective even as an arrow hits its target (Isa. 55:10-11). "I say to one, 'Go,' and he goes" (Matt. 8:9), as the Roman officer said to Jesus. How much more then must it be true when God speaks his Word. Deut. 31:21 says "this song will confront them as a witness" (for it will live unforgotten in the mouths of their descendants). So we may return to our original question as to whether it is Moses who is speaking here or whether we are really hearing the Word of God. For Moses is evidently, in all sincerity, speaking forth with the effective power of God issuing from his mouth.

Modern Western theologians often take for granted that their mode of thinking must be the only "right" one. Thus they may blandly declare that "Biblical Hebrew has no word for conscience," whereupon they deduce that "OT people were far less spiritually developed than was NT people." But such a conception ignores the reality upon which Moses took his stand. He did not need to use any word for conscience, for to Moses if a man or woman "walked humbly with God" (to use the language of a later prophet, Mic. 6:8) or believed in the reality, expressed later in the words of Ps. 51:17, "a broken and contrite heart, O God, you will not despise," the phrase "the Lord said unto Abraham" is actually a description of what "conscience" is to a believing person in every age. To have a conscience is to receive thankfully the indwelling presence and guidance of "the high and lofty one" into the heart of the "contrite and humble in spirit" (Isa. 57:15). We should note that the modern concept of conscience is the fruit of secular thinking, whereas the OT view is that conscience is the reception of a Word from the God of grace.

Moses' poem, therefore, while one small element in the whole story of Israel's escape from Egypt, the giving of the covenant, and the subsequent life in the wilderness wandering which has reached us today in the form of saga, is certainly not to be understood in terms of myth, even though myth itself is understandable in terms of "picture language." Metaphor often forms the primary language of much in the OT, and this is embodied in the poetic and imaginative thought of virtually all the OT prophets.

Northrop Frye, in *Words of Power,* accuses many literary critics of being "both ignorant and contemptuous of the mental processes that produce literature" (XVI). Unless we remember all this, we may misunderstand the argument employed in the Prologue to John's Gospel. Since it is the same Gospel that reports to us the claim of Jesus that "before Abraham was, I am" (John 8:58), we dare not deny that Christ, the eternal Word of grace, was revealed to the mind of Moses, even though it was only in the person of Jesus of Nazareth that "the Word became flesh" (John 1:14).

Consequently, we are reminded as we study Moses' Song that the song is basically about not Moses, not Israel, but God

11

himself. And so the Song of Moses falls into the category of revelation. An aspect of this is the awareness of God's purpose in his election of the "People of God." To quote Frye again (XIX), "The reader [of his *Words with Power*] will note a tendency . . . which has run through all my writing . . . to address myself less to a purely academic audience than to undergraduates and a nonspecialized public . . . . I know that this policy has confused even sympathetic academic reviewers, as well as driving others into all the hysterics of pedantry." I would suggest that this study of the Song of Moses may be seen to belong in this category of writing.

Because of this it is obvious that Moses was not caught up in a time warp. His words echo down the centuries, and again and again have taken ever new shape and substance. Seven hundred years after Moses' day, Isaiah can employ Moses' very words to call heaven and earth to witness (Isa. 1:2), for the heavens and the earth are still there maintaining and sustaining an Israel that by then had reached a very different level of culture and economy.

At Ps. 78:1-2 we have the poet beginning as Moses does, "Give ear, O my people, to my teaching *(torah)*; incline your ears to the words of my mouth. I will open my mouth in a parable *(mashal)*; I will utter dark sayings *(hidot)* from of old." *Mashal* here is not "parable" as we apply it to the parables of Jesus; we note that "dark sayings" qualifies it in parallel. The meaning of the term is "hidden ideas"; that is, they do not call a spade a spade, as with the riddles that Samson composed (Judg. 14:13-14). Together the nouns *mashal* and *hidot* describe what the biblical world set great store by, namely, picture language. Literalism is not a feature of OT revelation, whether conveyed in poetry or prose. Ezekiel's vision in ch. 1 of his prophecy is a good example of this fact. Ps. 78 tells the story of God's care for Israel in poetic pictorial terms — "He divided the sea and let them pass through it, and made the waters stand like a heap" (v. 13). In this manner the poet pictorializes how God was a "wall" unto his people when they needed him most.

Similarly, then, in our Song, Moses felt no embarrassment in calling God "The Rock" (Deut. 32:4).

Because of its pictorial quality, the Song became for any later generation and changing culture a "quarry" that was easily hewed, which has in fact been done throughout the whole of the Scriptures.

The normal form of Hebrew poetry is followed here, two lines at a time, the second balancing the first, expressing the idea of the couplet in two ways. The meter is usually, by our modern reckoning, 3:3.

> v. 2 May my teaching drop like the rain,
> my speech condense like the dew;
> like gentle rain on grass,
> like showers on new growth.

The word "teaching" *(leqah)* is peculiarly a "wisdom" term, such as we find used in the book of Proverbs, as is also the word *imre* as noted in v. 1. Scholars are now fully agreed that the inspiration behind our OT Wisdom Literature (e.g., Proverbs) comes largely from Egypt. Of course, Moses had been educated in Egypt, so he would know the content of the term he was using. Prov. 1:7; 9:10 remind us that "The fear of the LORD is the beginning of wisdom." *Leqah,* then, comes to mean almost our term "doctrine" (cf. Job 11:4; Isa. 29:24). Even as he studied Egyptian wisdom literature in his youth, Moses would surely ask himself, "Now, how would I say this in my own Hebrew language; how could I express this concept to my own Hebrew people?"

In Talmudic times, the tractate Bab. *Rosh Hashanah* 31a tells how, at the Musaf offering, the teaching of Moses was conveyed by singing his Song. What Moses has to say in it is so basic to faith that both the heavens and the earth are to pay heed. We note incidentally that Moses' *leqah* goes far beyond the issue of the salvation of individual souls, as some modern westerners

13

suppose to be God's primary concern. His Word is addressed to all creation (cf. Ps. 96:10-11).

Since "my teaching" is of God and is not "my own," it comes down gently from above, kindly, warningly, lovingly, as dew and gentle rain give life to crops (cf. Deut. 33:28; Ps. 72:16). God's rain does not flatten the grain, nor wash away the soil, but penetrates it to effect. We note, however, that dew is also the symbol of God's gracious care for his people. God gives them security, plenty, prosperity, all of which are elements of that *shalom* which is the content of his loving rule (cf. Gen. 27:28). "The word thus becomes an expression of God's saving will and universal design exalted over history" (Eichrodt, *Theology of the OT*, 2:74).

Yet, living in the Southern Hemisphere as I do, where the seasons are in reverse of the north in which biblical Palestine lies, I am reminded that the various natural phenomena are nothing more than symbols. The ultimate example of this is that where I live, since springtime occurs in October-November, there is no way that the spring flowers, or the baby bunnies (!) can lead us to believe in the Resurrection of Christ.

The "teaching" here is actually God's warning to Israel expressed in the theme that follows. It deals with the punishment to come, but only to lead in and through that judgment to the grace God bestows through the Covenant. Moses points a moral from the past experience of Israel in the wilderness wanderings, and from it warns his people about the future. He says in essence: "May my poem be as the fertilizing rain and dew upon hard human hearts!" Just as Christian youth have a right and a responsibility to know the meaning of their baptism, so the Israelites must be told the meaning of their election. As Ps. 103:7 puts it, "He made known his ways to Moses, his acts to the people of Israel." Moses' purpose, then, is to awaken trust in the living God. His theme is the character of God, not — as many Westerners would wish it — "*My* experience of God." His word *se'irim*, "gentle rain," is virtually a *hapax legomenon*, occurring nowhere else with this meaning. (The term is reflected at Ps.

72:6, where it is not the king's justice that is to descend upon Israel in this way, but God's — through the mouth of Israel's king.)

God's charge is a capital charge and so needs witnesses — heaven and earth. It takes the form of revelation, and so is expressed in solemn and terrible language. The occasion of the Song is an overwhelming one, one not to be taken lightly. Yet those very witnesses, as Isa. 55:10-11 unfolds the emphasis of the Song, reveal that, just as the rain and the snow are effective, "so shall my word be that goes out from my mouth; it shall not return to me empty, but it shall accomplish that which I purpose."

Later interpreters sought to exegete the term *leqah* by comparing it with the noun *torah*. The Targums of the Prophets in the 1st cent. A.D. identified such "teaching" with "law," and so with the Law of God given to Israel in the Pentateuch. Basing their argument on the fact that the hiphil (causative) form of the verb *yrh* means "to teach" (the verb from which we get the noun *torah*), the Aramaic translators accepted that only a living person can teach. Thus these translations or paraphrases seem to have argued that what came out of the teacher's mouth was a *revelation* of what was in his head. Thus *Torah* (the name of the first five books of the OT) was revelation from God himself.

Moses' word *leqah* is a noun derived from the verb "to take." It is revelation from God that Israel is to take, to receive, to accept. Hab. 3:2 builds similarly and most interestingly upon just such a divine "report." At 1 Cor. 11:23 we meet with the ultimate use of the term. There, in Paul's description of the Last Supper, we are urged by *word* to "take" the bread and the wine as gifts from God. God's revelation has always been by the Word of the LORD.

Moses then begins his Song with words of love and encouragement, and not of blame. Interestingly enough he employs the language and imagery of his day, for his vocabulary belongs also in the myths of the fertility cult of Ugarit, contemporary with himself. (See John Gray, *The Legacy of Canaan*, e.g.,

36). What Moses does, however, is to demythologize and poeti-
cize those concepts, and present them to God as vehicles for his
Word of life and love.

> v. 3 For I will proclaim the name of the LORD;
> ascribe greatness to our God!

The NRSV reads "*For* I will proclaim"; the Hebrew behind "for"
is *ki*. We note, first, that the LXX cannot be a true translation
with its "I have called upon . . ." The verb is not in the past
tense. Second, *ki* basically means "that" when it is preceded by
a verb, even if the verb is only understood. So we may translate:
"Remember, when I make mention of the name of the LORD,
you are to bless it." "You" here is not only heaven and earth, but
all Israel as well (cf. REB). This is because Yahweh's name describes and so reveals what Yahweh is in himself. Yahweh's name
differentiates him from all the divinities that have ever been
thought up by humankind. It is at Exod. 3 (a passage that must
have remained firmly in Moses' memory, to be passed on by
word of mouth until finally it found fixation in writing, probably in Solomon's day) that we read of Moses' experience of
God's presence at the burning bush, and so received from God
the content of his "name." Moses *heard* it (not *saw* it), as we
read at Exod. 3:12, in the words "I will be with you *(ehyeh
'immeka)*" when you go into Egypt. We note that "I will be" is
one word in Hebrew, and the same word as "I am." Thereafter
this promise, summarized at Exod. 3:14, reads "*ehyeh* has sent
me." At this point Gerhard von Rad, in his important *OT Theology* (1-78), warns us that there are many levels of the meaning
of this name *ehyeh*. "Whoever thinks he has discovered virgin
soil must discover at once that there are many more layers below
that." Yet clearly Yahweh is the God who reveals himself in
covenant with him whom he chooses to send, actually by going
with him on his mission, as we saw at Exod. 3:12. Moreover, in
revealing himself by name Yahweh is declaring that he is to be

understood in terms of personhood. The early author of Gen. 4:26 recognized that God, right from the beginning, was certainly not to be thought of as, for instance, "the ground of all being," so as to be a mere nameless energy or just an abstract idea. Otherwise God could not be called upon by his "name." Only persons have names, in the sense that human beings know what having a name implies. Rather, Yahweh is to be understood in terms of movement, growth, development, in that in this context the verb *hayah* means "become" rather than "be" (cf. Hos. 1:1).

How utterly different Yahweh is from the gods of Egypt. At Exod. 3 God is virtually saying to Moses, "You don't need to make up your mind to believe that a God such as Myself exists. This is because I have acted first in addressing you." The LORD has spoken. He has now chosen Moses, and in and through and with Moses he has thereby chosen all Moses' people, not just a select few. Thus "I am to be remembered," Moses discovered God to be saying to him, "throughout all generations" (Exod. 3:15). Consequently once they were rescued from Egypt and were living in covenant with Yahweh, the people Israel had to set forth on their "endless" pilgrimage, one which was to lead to commitment in mission to all peoples (Isa. 49:6). In his Anchor Bible commentary on Ruth Edward F. Campbell suggests that by the period of the judges the theology of the women at Ruth 4:14 is that "Israel" is the ideal, covenanted, socio-religious community (163), just as at v. 15 of Moses' Song Israel is Jeshurun, God's beloved people. That is why it is in *Israel* that Yahweh's name is to be celebrated. Ruth 4:14 reads: "Blessed be the LORD, who has not left you this day without next-of-kin; and may his name be renowned in Israel."

In reality it took Israel centuries to "hear" this "teaching" of Moses and to obey it. At Deut. 4:10 we learn that they prided themselves on God's choice, perhaps because they thought themselves to be more religious than other nations, or even more likable. But as vv. 36-37 of that chapter put it: "From heaven he made you hear his voice (cf. Exod. 34:5-6) to disci-

pline you . . . while you heard his words coming out of the fire
. . . because he loved your ancestors." What is more, God loved
them *to effect*. Centuries after the Song of Moses was first sung,
in the midst of the "fires" of the Babylonian exile, Israel — now
explicitly named as the Servant of Yahweh — is given a new
promise. It has arisen now out of the vitality of the promise of
God's love in Moses' day, love which had now created new
possibilities: "I will give you as a light to the nations, that my
salvation may reach to the end of the earth" (Isa. 49:6b). Election, it was now clear, was not based on any kind of favoritism,
as anti-Semites have alleged to this day. Election is for service;
yet in that service the elect finds salvation.

The second line declares: "Ascribe *greatness* to our God,"
another noun evidently basic to the language of the Song. This
word is used most often with the idea of "loftiness," what today
we would term "transcendence." God's is a greatness therefore
that sets him apart from all the gods of mankind. Yet the concept
of transcending is so overwhelming to our puny human intelligence that it is revealed to us gently and kindly like the falling
of the dew. For it is the greatness of divine love which God
thereupon asks Israel to reflect to all mankind. Thus the rabbis
say of this verse, "When one ascribes greatness to God one has
begun to do the will of God" (cf. Ps. 29:1).

First then Moses says, "I will proclaim. . . ." The completion
of the line follows as, "Ascribe *ye* (plural) greatness to our God."
Yahweh is *ehyeh*, the living God, and now he is called *our* God.
So Moses is actually praying here: "May my preaching be creative; may it give new life to dead souls in Israel." This is a prayer
which we see God answering as the story of Israel unfolded.

Yet "to proclaim the name" has a still more profound meaning. It is one we meet with in the Lord's Prayer: "Hallowed be
thy name." The NJB has a footnote here to suggest that its
translation "Oh, tell the greatness of our God" is an exordium
addressed to the whole created world. The clause would then
be a petition to God to exert himself in action in history, that
is, in human experience. Ezek. 36:23 shows that this may be the

likeliest meaning of the clause, as does also John 12:28. Thus we can make bold to say that the gospel found in the NT does not "begin" with the Gospels, but rather begins with Moses. It is of course possible and permissible to read the Bible in a meditative fashion so that it becomes a stimulus to our own faith and experience of God's presence in our lives. "But when that happens, the thoughts are our own and are not to be confused with the meaning of what we have read" (G. B. Caird, *The Language and Imagery of the Bible,* 40).

The name of God, Yahweh, is thus a "theophany" of the divine being to the mind of human beings (see G. A. F. Knight, "Theophany," 4:827). As a theophany the name may be regarded as the "alter ego" of its owner. If you profane God's name, you profane God himself (Lev. 19:12). Again, God's name is the "vehicle" that God gives to Moses for the priests to use when they lay God's blessing upon his people: "So they shall put my name on the Israelites, and I will bless them" (Num. 6:27).

Since this is what the OT keeps saying, that God speaks and acts interrelatedly with Israel, in and through historical events, Israel thus becomes *the* historical fact that compels us to recognize the "factuality" of God. Israel, in fact, becomes the "proof" of the existence of God.

Moreover, this is true despite the reality that God's name is "wonderful" *(peli'i),* "secret," "belonging within the eternity that is hidden from our eyes" (Judg. 13:18) — yet God reveals himself to Abraham and to Moses by disclosing his secret name (Gen. 17:1; Exod. 6:2; Hans Bietenhard, "ὄνομα," *TDNT* 5:255), the essence of himself. This (to us) inconceivable paradox is made evident through the Bible's use of parabolic and picture language. Even while Yahweh "dwells in heaven" (Deut. 26:15) he chooses a place to cause his name to dwell there (e.g., 12:11; 14:23). What a mighty task Moses is called upon to execute then — he has to "proclaim the name of the LORD," and invite his people to do likewise.

Finally, how fascinating it is to trace the ongoing movement of the living Word. We note that the present-day popular hymn

"How Great Thou Art" is now seen to be in the direct line of that movement from the Song of Moses as it flowers in the worship of the Church today.

> v. 4 The Rock, his work is perfect,
>   and all his ways are just.
> A faithful God, without deceit,
>   just and upright is he.

Verse 3 had ended with the word "God." Verse 4 resumes with a *casus pendens* referring to him as "the Rock." Toward the end of their journey through the wilderness Moses and his people crossed the desolate wasteland south of the Dead Sea and entered the hill country that borders the area of the modern kingdom of Jordan. From the wilderness period onward Israel's imagination was constantly stirred by the illustration that Moses' generation had received when they recognized the steadfastness of the Rock City they met with there. (We should note that the opposite of "rock" is "sand.") The fact that the Rock City emerges from a sandy waste is striking. We should remember this fact when we examine the NT parable of the house built upon the rock (Matt. 7:24-27). Moses was thus the first to use the illustration of Petra to suggest the faithfulness, the consistency, the reliability of God.

After wandering for years in the open wilderness, even at times in sheer desert, the Israelites were struck by the strange sight of a group of human families living in complete safety in caves hewn out of the living rock. A thousand years later, when the OT was still in the process of formation, this strange collection of homes had grown and developed to be the city known as *Sela* (Hebrew for "rock"), the capital city of the Nabatean kingdom, called by the Romans *Petra*. Being so close to Judah it remained in the minds of the writers of Judg. 1:36; 2 Kgs. 14:7; Isa. 16:1. It is employed quite naturally in the same sense as in the Song of Moses at 2 Sam. 22:2, 32, a psalm that appears also in the Psalter as Ps. 18.

20

Moses employs the figure of Rock six times in his Song. As G. B. Caird puts it, "God speaks to man in similitudes" or parables (cf. Ps. 78:2; Hos. 12:10), "and man has no language but analogy for speaking about God" (144).

Remember that virtually all the language used of God in the Hebrew of the OT from Moses onward is metaphorical in nature. Because of this an illiterate people can usually grasp the significance of the gospel best, especially if it is presented to them in OT terms.

The term "rock" later becomes a picture of the abstract concept of *hesed*, a word which, although it does not occur in our text, is the OT prophets' term for the unshakable, loyal love of Yahweh. It emphasizes well what is demonstrated in English by the two words used by the NRSV in Ps. 136, "steadfast love." That the term *hesed* was so long misunderstood arises from the fact that toward the end of the OT period the LXX translation sought to rid itself of much of this metaphorical language. By way of illustration we can imagine a teacher, standing before a blackboard, asking the class "Tell me, what do the theological terms atonement, justification, reconciliation, perversity, salvation mean?" And when the class remains silent, with his chalk he draws a picture of each of these terms on the blackboard, for each of them is expressed in OT picture language.

The picture of God as Rock conveys to the unscientific human mind the idea of timelessness. The Rock had been there before Moses' day. In fact, it had been there from the "beginning" and so would be there at the "end."

Then again, because of the covenant which Yahweh had bestowed upon Israel at Sinai, Israel — the other party to the covenant — was intended by their show of *hesed* toward God to reflect thereafter that same steadfast love to others. They were to be "a priest to the nations" (cf. Exod. 19:6). That is why Abraham was elected to be a rock to succeeding generations (Isa. 51:1-2), and why even ordinary Israelites were elected to be a rock to shelter the weary and oppressed among mankind (Isa. 32:2).

An aspect of God's *hesed* is his *emunah,* "faithfulness." The term conveys the idea of reliability, because of its root meaning "firm," "unshakable." Yet, as Eduard Schweizer declares in his commentary on Colossians (Minneapolis: Augsburg and London: SPCK, 1982), it has the "character of mystery; it can never be deduced with necessity, but only received as a gift" (35; cf. Ps. 119:43). Deut. 32:4 is probably the first recorded usage of this noun *emunah,* whose meaning is best grasped when it is connected with the idea of Rock.

The Pentateuch was translated into Greek, the language of the Roman Empire and of commerce as far east as Persia, about 300 or 250 B.C., some nine hundred years after Moses first uttered this Song. The faith of Israel had developed greatly over those centuries, particularly as a result of having to "go through the fires" of the Babylonian Exile (587-538; cf. Dan. 3). The first band of returnees, who reached Jerusalem soon after 538 only to find it in ruins, had clearly learned much from their experience of God's love during the exile. This first group now saw themselves as "the New Israel," called of God to implement the challenge of Isa. 49:6; Mic. 6:8 (see G. A. F. Knight, *The New Israel*). They became an "underground" movement once Haggai and Zechariah gained the leadership, and remained so a century later because of the prestige of Ezra and Nehemiah. Their theological position was to be revived only with the coming of Christianity.

Yet all throughout that long period, as Moses foresaw, Yahweh the Rock was to remain faithful to Israel, even when Israel misunderstood what that faithfulness entailed for them (see later in our Song). For Israel's response at many periods was one of unfaithfulness. Israel had, of course, the free will to be unfaithful. It is foolish, said the church father Origen, to suggest that in whatever God foreknows there is no freedom, for it is precisely the acts of free will that God foreknows. Thus God can take up Israel's rebelliousness into his loving plan for his people, for as Paul learned from Moses God "is able to accomplish abundantly far more than all we can ask or imagine" (Eph. 3:20).

22

At Deut. 32:3 we looked at the basic revelation of his name that God made known to Moses in the incident of the burning bush through the original Hebrew that Moses spoke. The LXX's interpretation of "I will be (or become) with you" (Heb. *ehyeh 'immeka*) at Exod. 3:12 is, however, something quite else. It is in Greek *ego eimi ho ōn* (v. 14). These words can only mean "I am the existent one." Lost, therefore, is the personal, creative, loving movement of God to man, and in its place is a mere impersonal, philosophical concept of the nature of God derived from Greek philosophy.

With this verse as a warning, then, we must on every occasion scrutinize the Greek translation of Moses' words, always remembering that it was made nearly a thousand years after the Song was first sung. We must also remember that the LXX was penned by scholars who as fallible human beings were blissfully unaware that they were but children of their day and age. Ultimately we are to remember also that it was the LXX that became the Bible of the gentile Church, for of course the Hebrew Bible remained a closed book to all but a few enthusiasts among those in the early Church who fashioned for us today the theology of the Church catholic.

The Hebrew word for Rock here is *tsur*. In Greek it should be *petra*, but after its fashion, ignoring all "pictorial theology," the LXX has merely *theos*, "God." By doing so the Greek Version obstructs the manner in which the significance of "rock" grows and develops throughout the Hebrew Bible — and the NT! (cf. Matt. 16:18; 1 Cor. 10:4). But "rock" exemplifies the Hebrew genius for employing metaphor, parable, poetry, and picture language to express what is otherwise inexpressible by mortals. As Isa. 55:8 puts it, "For my thoughts are not your thoughts, nor are your ways my ways, says the LORD." How expressive it is to say that Abraham is the "second-story" rock resting on the cornerstone of the temple (Isa. 51:1-2). This particular picture seems to be the key to interpreting what Christ meant when he called foolish Peter "rock" (Matt. 16:18). The Greek spirit has remained alive to this day and is the chief implement employed by secular humanists to deny the significance of this medium of revelation in the Scriptures as a whole.

The rock on which Jerusalem stood — and stands, the rock on which the temple was built, through the centuries took over the significance of the title which Moses had given to God, thereby producing a medium for a theology of incarnation to develop. This we discover at Rom 9:32f.; 1 Pet. 2:8, both of which quote Isa. 8:14, yet point to 28:16. God as Rock develops to be the image of holy wrath and at the same time that of gracious faithfulness. God as Rock ever remains faithful to his creature mankind-under-judgment. God is the God of justice in *all* his ways, that is, in every aspect of his divine rule. And that goes beyond mankind. God's justice covers even earthquakes, diseases "nature red in tooth and claw," and so *all* calamities that mankind must face in this world.

Again we note that while "Rock" seems to represent something quite impersonal, yet Moses can say that God's *work* is perfect. What God does is always complete. Such is the meaning of the NT's declaration that God's "work" in Christ is complete (cf. John 17:4). God is the living, active, creative God, who is totally faithful to what his name represents. The Hebrew term *emunah* here (RSV "faithfulness") may be used to describe, for example, a perennial spring of water, or an ancient vine that bears fruit without fail each year, or a city gatepost that is solid and sure. God is *tsaddiq* (NRSV "just"), a word which means more than merely "righteous," because to modern ears the phrase "a righteous person" can sound quite objectionable. The word today has acquired the notion of self-righteous. It is to Isaiah, in the whole sixty-six chapters of that long book, that we owe the fullest interpretation of Moses' term, for *tsaddiq* in Isaiah means self-giving, loving, compassionate, caring (see George A. F. Knight, "Is Righteous Right?", 1). Consequently "deceit" (*'awel;* RSV "iniquity") means the opposite of what *tsaddiq* pictorializes for us. Once again the LXX has not grasped the meaning, for it translates *'awel* by *adikia,* "nonrighteousness," and so relates the negative to a misunderstanding of *tsaddiq.*

God, says Moses, remains the same yesterday, today, and forever (cf. Rev. 1:8). He is the divinity *(el)* of *emunah*, consistency, reliability, unshakableness, trustworthiness. Consequently it is that aspect of God which must then be the opposite of iniquity — God is "without deceit" (thus the terrible denunciation of human iniquity at Hab. 1:12).

To sum up, we learn that God as Rock is the God of *hesed* (a word which, as we noted, does not occur in the Song of Moses). *Hesed* is the constant, steadfast love that God *acts* toward Israel, the people of the Covenant, and so reveals his love in his ongoing relationship to Israel. *Tsaddiq* speaks of God's saving *acts* and covenant faithfulness (cf. Jer. 50:7; Isa. 41:2, 10; 45:8; 51:5). Accordingly, we can see how God's justice *(mishpat)* and his salvation are linked together by means of the Covenant (Ps. 25:6ff.; 76:9; 82:2f.; 103:6ff.). *Mishpat* is the legal claim which belongs to the poor and needy. This is acknowledged here when we hear that "all his ways are *mishpat*," so that even as God cares for all his creation, the poor particularly belong in the "all." Thus God's *mishpat* ("justice") actually springs from his mercy and grace, while the figure of Rock shows that this is consistently so (Ps. 105:5-9). "Then Bildad the Shuhite answered: . . . 'You who tear yourself in your anger — shall the earth be forsaken because of you, or the rock be removed out of its place?'" (Job 18:1, 4).

The regular employment of the term "rock" throughout the OT, taken as it is from the natural world, leads us to acknowledge that God's faithfulness is not limited to his creature mankind. God is faithful to all of his creation. When "the mountains are cast into the midst of the seas" — that is, the whole area of natural evils such as earthquakes and droughts, epidemics and death — God is still the same, even there and then. None of God's creatures is beyond his care (Ps. 103; 104:21; 147:9; Job 37:5) — the whole realm of botany, zoology, physics, and astrophysics. It is natural that God should seek to reveal himself as such. That is why, again and again, we hear that God *acts* "for his name's sake," so often in fact that there is no need to quote chapter and verse.

25

Finally, since God is responsible for both good and evil (Isa. 45:7) we come to the awesome awareness that God must carry in his own heart the pain that his creative purpose brings about. The prophets and the book of Job find the Song of Moses to be a basic quarry for this revelation, so it is no surprise to find St. Paul also quarrying at this point in the Song.

> v. 5 Yet his degenerate children have dealt falsely
>   with him,
>   a perverse and crooked generation.

Verse 4 ended with the emphatic pronoun "he," God. Now we come to "they," Israel, and are shown the reverse of the steadfast love and caring actions of the God of the Covenant. It takes two to make a covenant. All Moses had to do was to mediate between the two parties. He had begun his Song by calling upon heaven and earth to witness, first to the immensity of the greatness of God. But now the heavens and the earth are to witness to the immensity of the perversity of God's partner to the Covenant. If heaven and earth are to hear, and of course "abide," then what is said is for the ears of all generations, including our own today.

Bound by the Sinai covenant, Israel is to do justice and to be faithful to God, being called to be a kingdom of priests so as to fulfil this calling (Exod. 19:6). Inherent in that calling, as Deutero-Isaiah later recognized, is "to do to others what I have done to you." "I have taken you by the hand and kept you; I have given you as a covenant to the people [of the earth], a light to the nations, to open the eyes that are blind, to bring out the prisoners from the dungeon" (even as God had brought Israel out of the horrors of slavery in Egypt), "from the prison those who sit in darkness" (Isa. 42:6-7). Clearly we hear an echo of this at Luke 4:16-18. From his action at the Red (or "Reed") Sea God had revealed himself to be the loving, serving God, both of Israel and therefore through Israel of all humanity. This then is what Moses seeks to emphasize at this point — but, as we see, to no avail. Despite forty years of loving correction and education in the wilderness, this covenant people was planning to cross the river Jordan into the Promised Land in a mood of rebellion and of rejection of their adoption into God's plan for his world.

Here then, in the Hebrew of Moses' original dictum, we have the concept of a radical corruption of human nature. Israel, he says, is 'iqqesh, "twisted" (NRSV "perverse"). The RSV speaks of their "blemish" (mum), which is well described later by the prophet Hosea. An apple on whose outer skin a blemish shows is one in which a worm has taken up residence at its heart, and is eating up the fruit from within. So Israel has become rotten through and through. God's people have "wrestled themselves" (petaltol) out of the bonds of the Covenant, or as Isaiah put it centuries later, "They have rebelled against me" (pesha'; Isa. 1:2), not just against the bonds of the Covenant but against God as Person (cf. also Matt. 17:17).

Since the language is that of horticulture (e.g., "blemish"), we are shown that God is not the root cause of Israel's corruption. A blemish shows itself on the skin of a fruit, until its source is revealed in the core as putrid matter. This then is not a picture of original sin. In Proverbs we find that 'iqqesh ("corrupt") is frequently the opposite of "blameless." To be perverse and crooked reveals the total and deliberate rejection of love, even as the person who is loved remains self-righteous and sure of his own integrity. The reality of new life wrought by God's forgiveness and grace is illustrated in the NT where amomos ("unblemished," the absence of defects in sacrificial animals) is used to describe the perfect piety of those believers who are obligated by membership in the covenant people. Consequently Yahweh is just and right (v. 4) in punishing and so educating his people, for his handling of them is an aspect of his loving purpose for them and of his care for and creative love toward them.

Before leaving v. 5 we may wonder whether the NJB, in following the centuries later Greek and Samaritan Versions of the Song by reading "those he fathered without blemish," is not introducing a dogmatic interpretation foreign to Moses' thought. The NJB offers us a footnote which declares "Israel is of noble birth, being born of Yahweh; his degeneration is his own doing." The first half of this statement is refuted by the Hebrew of v. 10: "he found him in a desert land" (so RSV). We should compare this with the archetypal story of the birth of Cain the murderer, who was born *et* ("*with [the help of]*") *Yahweh* (Gen. 4:1).

> v. 6　Do you thus repay the LORD,
> 　　　O foolish and senseless people?
> 　　Is not he your father, who created you,
> 　　　who made you and established you?

The Hebrew of line 1 begains with the emphatic question: "Is it the LORD whom you are thus requiting?" "Folly in Israel" (from the same root as "foolish") is regarded at Gen. 34:7 as sexual promiscuity, at Judg. 20:6 as sexual violence, and at Jer. 29:23 as plain adultery. Adultery is an act that marks the deliberate rejection of the "marital" fellowship that Israel ought to have displayed toward God within the bond of the Covenant. That is why "going awhoring after other gods" is regularly viewed as Israel's basic sin (cf. Hos. 1–3). It marks a rejection of love. Martin Noth regards this "folly" as stemming from the unwritten customary law in the period of the judges, becoming "serious disorderly conduct" — such as we witness today in the behavior of some football fans. So seriously do the biblical writers take this word *nabal* that even a century before Christ Ben Sira applied the term to the Samaritans, regarding them actually as dangerous schismatics. "Requite" (*gamal*) is thus better rendered by "recompense" with all the violent insolence that is conveyed by the term. What Moses is pointing out is that the *whole* of Israel's common life was under the rule of God.

"Foolish" (*nabal*) here is not a reference to stupidity or clownishness. It represents the opposite of "the fear of the

Lord." Thus it describes that state of impiousness which is what Jesus, quoting Isa. 32:6, called the sin against the Holy Spirit. The word thus describes a tragic alteration in the personality. Paul can therefore use Moses' word to reveal in reverse the difference between his own *worldly* generation and the new generation of Christians which he describes as those who "shine as stars in the world" (Phil. 2:15).

"Father" here means primarily "progenitor," the one who created you *(qanah)*. Yet the noun is distinctly personalized since the whole nexus of ideas in this verse is infused with love.

Much ink has been spilled seeking to reach a consensus on the meaning of this verb *qanah*. Does it mean "to give birth to" and so "to beget," "to father," or does it mean "to create?" (see Peter Walters, *The Text of the Septuagint*). Basically the verb *qanah* is as vague as is the English "to get" — whether by pro-creation and so creation, adoption; or "to come by," by loan, stealing, or otherwise. The emphasis of Deut. 32:10, however, seems to suggest that the words here "your father, who created you *(qanah)*, who made you *('asah)*, and established you *(kun)*" are to be interpreted as declaring that Yahweh adopted a found-ling and then "made" him what he meant him to become, a child of God; God "established" him in the new relationship to himself of covenant and care. Thus, although God did not create Israel (the verb would then be *bara'*, as at Gen. 1:1) or give him birth as his natural or biological father (Moses would leave such an idea to be held by some of Israel's neighbors about their relationship to their national god), yet God did indeed "create" Israel by grace from being that destitute foundling to becoming his "firstborn son" (Exod. 4:22). Love is creative of love in the other party, and love is no less than life itself.

We should note that, as with the verb *bara'*, God is always the subject of *qanah* when it is specifically not used of a human being merely "getting" something. We find this at Gen. 4:1 (which should be compared with Matt. 1:20-21), in the creation of a human baby, and at Prov. 8:22ff. of God's relationship to his "daughter," Wisdom personified. At Gen. 14:19, 22, in a

29

poem as ancient as Moses' Song, God *qanah*-ed the earth and the heavens. In every case, then, including that of Israel itself, in a basic sense *qanah* virtually always occurs with God as Creator.

Rashbam the Jewish sage, in the Talmudic commentary on Deuteronomy, paraphrases by saying "born out of Egypt." In this way the "birth" concept emphasizes that even God underwent the pains of childbirth, even though it is the masculine "father" that occurs here. For a discussion of this reference to Egypt, see v. 10 below.

Moses now preaches the good news of God to his contemporary generation in the wilderness. He begins his indictment gradually and gently (cf. Deut. 32:2). It is the human stupidity of unbelief on which he puts his finger, remembering, it would seem, the weakness of our human flesh. Moses begins almost reproachfully, but we soon hear a note of sorrow, one that exhibits (as we learn from Hos. 11:1-4) a sob in the voice of God. Tenderness and pity prevail over severity, so the main thrust here is one of warning and not condemnation. In the Hebrew text, this tenderness is expressed by the use of the singular: "*your* father . . . created *you* . . . made *you* and formed *you*." Here then is a presentation of the theology of creation without parallel in the OT; later, it becomes the basis of the Song of Hannah (1 Sam. 2:1-10) and then of the Song of Mary (Luke 1:46-55). Moreover, as a song it is meant to be sung. The cantor in the synagogue sings it to this day. This is important, for many declare today that "a congregation gets its theology largely from its hymnbook."

Moses' Song shows that God's action in creation and in salvation are one, as does Deutero-Isaiah at Isa. 43:1. Too many Christians today, who have not learned to put the OT back into the Bible, put their emphasis upon one of these acts of God to the detriment of the other. Moses actually calls such people "witless."

Moses lived several centuries before the birth of Buddha. Buddhism has no god, yet it is hailed as the great religion of love. Moses never says as much about Yahweh, on the ground that — as Moses would agree — there is no such thing as love apart from the living being who does the loving. For love is not a sentiment; it is an action. So Moses sings of the creator God, the living God, nowhere deifying love as a thing in itself.

Within his plan of love, then, God "made" you, Israel. This verb is rendered in the LXX by *eplase*, "pleated," "shaped," as of clay, as a synonym of *poieo*: God "handicrafted" you in the whole historical process from Egypt onward (Isa. 44:2; Ps. 119:73). "Established" *(kun)* again refers to setting your feet on the way he has chosen for you to go. This reminds us therefore of a basic element in the theology of infant baptism. So God has handled and cared for you in love as you passed through childhood to adulthood (Hos. 11:1-4; Jer. 3:19; 31:20; Deut. 8:5). Accordingly Isa. 64:7-8, building upon this verse, can pictorialize God's creative handling of his people as being like that of a potter who works the clay to the shape he has had in mind from the beginning.

The Bible is not concerned first about mankind (far less about "me"!); it is first of all about God. The Bible offers us revelation of God, of the God of creative love. The various Reformation confessions that have come down to us are thus not afraid to acknowledge their astonishment that in Moses' theology the ever-living and ever-loving God is first known as the one who first creates and then sustains in being those peoples and nations, including Israel, who persistently oppose his authority and rebel against his will for their good. It is to be noted, therefore, that nowhere does Moses call God himself "good." We saw at Deut. 32:4 that God is *tsaddiq* and *yashar*, "just" and "right" (RSV). It would not have been possible for Moses to have known even that much of God had it not been for the covenant made at Sinai. Israel was enabled to know God as such and then use these words to describe him only because of Moses' initial interpretation upon the series of divine acts of redemption when God brought his people out of Egypt. So "just" and "right" "in *all* his ways" are not adjec-

31

tives used of an abstract concept of God. God had been just *to* Israel, and faithful *to* his rebellious people. These Hebrew terms, belonging as they do within the covenant relationship, seek to express almost a "movement" in love toward their human recipient, because they are coming from the "living" God. In similar manner, then, "good" is not to be understood as "morally" perfect. God is good *for* Israel — a frequent use of the term *tob*. Thus God shows himself to be both self-effacing and unassuming.

This emphasis is clearly seen in Israel's literature. At Exod. 2:2 we read that when Moses was born his mother saw that her baby was *tob*. The NEB renders "She saw what a *fine* child he was." The RSV attempts to be more literal with "goodly." But when we remember that the book of Exodus is not primarily about Moses but is about God, we recognize that the author of that chapter, knowing what Moses later on did for both God and Israel, certainly was not interested to tell us that Moses was "a good little boy," but that in the providence of God Moses was "good for" God's plan of redemption.

Again at Gen. 1:31 we read "God saw everything that he had made, and indeed, it was very good" *(tob)*. Morally good? Of course not. The potency of the term might then be expanded to read "good for his cosmic plan of creative love."

We understand then why the OT, following Moses, very seldom calls God "good." There is no need to do so. God's goodness is clearly seen in all the loving care he takes of Israel, in being "just and right" *for* his beloved people (Deut. 32:4).

As Abraham J. Heschel puts it in *The Prophets,* "Never do we hear the words, 'Hear, O Israel, the LORD our God is perfect,' for such would be a mere human evaluation of God. Always it is his work that is perfect, what God does for the salvation of mankind, his actions in history, his self-revelation, his own initiative as he acts first in grace. This is how his essence is identified with his ways" (274). Heschel continues, "And now, says Moses, Israel is God's work. Thus, in the sense of like father, like son, Israel is meant to exhibit God's moral demands, and in the language of the later book of Leviticus: 'Be ye holy, even as I am holy.'"

However, it is not God's fault that the people find themselves in a mess. On his part, God created Israel, was their Father, and was faithful to his Covenant promise. It was they who were "foolish and senseless," in that they had lost "the fear of the LORD." "Fear him who . . . has power (NRSV "authority") to cast into hell" (Luke 12:5).

> v. 7 Remember the days of old,
>   consider the years long past;
>   ask your father, and he will inform you;
>   your elders, and they will tell you.

"Remember" is a singular verb, used to address all Israel as one corporate entity, just as we can speak today of Uncle Sam or of Holy Mother Church. The verb summons Moses' hearers — as did the prophets in later centuries, and as did Jesus in his "sermon" on the meaning of the Last Supper (1 Cor. 11:24) — to think historically, and not to fall into the trap of thinking merely as "the now generation" is inclined to do. Although the editors of Deuteronomy place the Song of Moses at the end of their book, and just before Moses' death, the whole book develops a theology of remembering arising from this verse. That every generation in ages to come was to do so points to the "quarry" nature of the Song. For Israel's memory could go back, through the terrible years of the oppression in Egypt to the stories it had rehearsed by word of mouth about Abraham, Isaac, Jacob, and Joseph. Deuteronomy 32:4 had spoken of the "work" of God; his work is what is seen in history. Interestingly, Moses' command is reversed at Isa. 63:11. There it is God who remembers Moses the man who is himself an element in these mighty works. Moreover, these, including the person of Moses, are declared to be of eschatological significance, that is, they belong in 'olam ("eternity"). So we see the link between our

Song and the words of Jesus addressed to those Sadducees who had lost the OT significance of the OT word 'olam: "Have you not *read* [in the Song of Moses] what was said to *you:* "I am (not 'was') the God of Abraham . . ." (Matt. 22:31-32).

"The days of old" is therefore an ambivalent translation. It seems to be paralleled by "years long past" (RSV "many generations") and so may actually be correct as it stands here. Hebrew *dor wa-dor* (literally, "generation and generation") can often refer to remote time in the past, and may thus explain the phrase here "days of 'olam." But Hebraic thinking about space and time is different from that of the Greeks such as is embedded in our Western philosophy of civilization. First, in Hebraic thinking space and time are but two aspects of the same thing. That explains why in Talmudic times (the early Christian centuries) 'olam can even be translated "the world." Did it have this meaning in essence in Moses' day? Of course Moses seems to have had no explicit concept of life beyond the grave. Second, and on the other hand, not only did OT thought keep the concepts of time and space in close contiguity, it also considered time and eternity as being as closely connected as the two sides of a coin. "Eternity," for us mortals, therefore, will not begin merely after our death. Eternity is present now, though being on the back of the coin it is unseen by the eyes of mortals. Yahweh is the God of eternity ('olam), the back of the coin. The RSV translates 'olam at v. 40 by "I live forever." Yahweh is thus the God of yesterday, and of all our yesterdays, the God of our history. God has so bound himself in relationship to the world that he and they move through time and space together. Thus God is ever present at all our "times"; in fact, eternity is ever with us, and each of our "moments" has eschatological significance. We are reminded of T. S. Eliot's poem: ". . . the moment of the rose and the moment of the yew tree are of equal duration." This means again that the life of each one of us is of infinite importance, for what we do now actually creates our eternal fate. "Eternity" is therefore pictured like a rainbow arch that spreads over our life and times, every strand of the rainbow overhead being equidistant from mankind's life on earth, as much in the remote future as in the remote past. In Jesus' parable of the last judgment (Matt. 25:31-46), uttered within the flow not of Platonic thought but of Mosaic, we are shown pictorially that every decision we make on earth, in time, is in reality a last and final decision, bearing within it our own last judgment.

Again with reference to "the days of old," the Hebrew word *yom* can mean much more than a period of twenty-four hours. It can mean even a "moment" of divine visitation or judgment, as for instance a battle in which God has clearly been present. Thus the "day" of Midian is how the later prophet at Isa. 9:4 can look back upon what Judg. 7:15-23 describes as a day of victory, when Yahweh led Gideon to defeat the Midianites decisively. In the same way Isaiah could look forward to what Yahweh would do "in that day," "his" day (Isa. 2:11-12; Ps. 110:5) — the day of God's wrath! Keeping in mind this context to the word "day," we are to see that Moses invites Israel to think back even beyond history, when "the days of old" enfolded even the beginning of creation (Gen. 1; Isa. 51:16).

The root of the noun *olam* conveys the idea of "hiddenness," and so of what is hidden from the eyes of mortals. It is in such manner that we are not able to see both sides of a coin at once. A term allied to *olam* is Heb. *aharit,* a noun formed from the root *ahar,* meaning "behind," "after," "back." While it can mean any of these in a physical sense, the term can also convey the idea of "backside," "back of the coin," and so theologically speaking of "ultimate outcome." Psalm 37:37-38, for example, says "There is *aharit* for the peaceable," while the wicked is to be cut off. Cf. also Gen. 49:1; Deut. 8:16; Jer. 23:20; 30:24; Mic. 4:1. Although this term does not occur in the Song of Moses, elsewhere it is employed to supplement and clarify *olam.* In a word, then, it is the "eschatological significance" of events in Israel's past to which Moses points here and not to their mere historicity, in that they are "the mighty acts of God." We may say that to Moses time is sacramental, in that it is the vehicle of the activity of the eternal God. All this, then, "your elders" are to *higgid* (NRSV "inform") to the next generation; having "stood before" *(nagad)* the LORD themselves, they must, as inherent in belonging in Israel, then "proclaim" it to their children (see v. 46).

Later writers take up the advice Moses gives here, that parents should teach their children to understand history in this sacramental sense (e.g., Deut. 6:7) and that children be encouraged to ask their elders about the past. The incident where the twelve-year-old Jesus does just this in the Jerusalem temple thus fits with the biblical tradition (Luke 2:41-52).

After the new generation has learned to "remember the days of old," there follows the first fundamental element in Israel's relationship to Yahweh, which is *obedience* (Gerhard von Rad). This command of God pervades the later book of Deuteronomy, and through it the whole biblical revelation. It is *not* obedience therefore for a parent, Jew or Christian, to avoid teaching his or her children the meaning of their baptism or bar mitzvah, declaring, "I want my children to choose their own religion for themselves when they grow up." How can they ever make a decision if they have never been taught the options?

> v. 8 When the Most High apportioned the nations,
> when he divided humankind,
> he fixed the boundaries of the peoples
> according to the number of the sons of God.

That the Song of Moses is ancient shows itself in several places where the background of the period before the judges is described quite naturally. The title "Most High" for Yahweh *('elyon)* was common to the Ugaritic literature of the period, and Elyon was also the name of the pre-Davidic god of Jerusalem. We notice the title also at Gen. 14:18, where Abraham met with Melchizedek king of Salem, called in this ancient oral tradition "priest of God Most High." This title for Yahweh was used only sporadically in later years, especially when the writer sought to emphasize the "ancientness" of Israel's faith; for example, we find it in the Song of David, 2 Sam. 22:14 (= Ps. 18:13); and then more frequently in the age of the Priestly writer(s), at Num. 24:16; Isa. 14:14 and in many psalms. By then another emphasis was being made as well, that of the universality of Yahweh: "He is LORD of heaven and earth and God of all nations."

Here as Most High God, Yahweh is Israel's God before covenantal history began. In primeval times Yahweh had given to each nation a "place," a space to call its own. This he did by separating humankind (RSV "the sons of men") into national groupings, each group receiving its "inheritance" (RSV). As the Polynesian peoples put it today, the gods gave each nation of people room to "stand tall." We note then a basic fact about Yahweh's plan for his humanity: Yahweh works by separating. In the beginning God separated light from darkness (Gen. 1:4); he separated the primal waters into two portions (v. 7); he separated the day from the night (v. 14). Then God differentiated the various species of animal life. So here, when God "fixed the boundaries of the peoples" he was evidently giving each nation the right to be itself and to appreciate and foster its own culture and language. Thus God intended good to derive from his plan of dispersing (NEB) or separating the nations after they had left off seeking a spurious unity in their attempts to create a world religion through an "ascent to God" (Gen. 11:8; Acts 17:26). Even today the Buddhist myth attracts many in the West, in which the various religions of mankind are shown to be various ascents of the one mountain, whereupon all meet together at the top.

The word "religion," of course, never occurs in the Bible. The closest we can render this modern word into Biblical Hebrew is to translate it "Baal worship." The Bible, of which Moses is a voice, deals basically not with religion at all but with revelation through the Word. Here then in this verse we are shown the close relationship between revelation and the election of Israel.

The LORD then fixed *yasseb*, the boundaries of the peoples. He left them no doubt as to where they belonged. For he was their God too, no matter what other gods they chose to worship (cf. Ps. 82:1; 89:5-8). Balancing this concept, however, is the view that the national gods or ideologies of mankind have a legitimate function within their own assigned territory, similar to Yahweh's function within Israel (cf. Judg. 11:24). What makes a nation cohere as a cultural group is their very own well-thought-out ideology and mode of life. If this is a true understanding of the thought of Moses, then it sheds an important light on Israel's mission-in-covenant to the nations, and so of the Church today as it encounters the religions and ideologies of peoples now being uprooted from their "God-given" boundaries and finding themselves rootless in the large cities of the world.

At Jer. 10:7 the prophet calls Yahweh "King of the nations," yet "in all their kingdoms there is no one like you." At Rev. 15:3-4 this last book of the Bible links the Song of Moses with the Song of the Lamb, declaring "All nations will come and worship before you."

We can see then that the Table of Nations in Gen. 10 recognizes that God's action is a divine ordering and is not a punishment, as some suggest of Gen. 11, falsely exegeting the fate of the generations of the tower of Babel.

Lying behind the NRSV reading "apportioned the nations" is the Hebrew noun *nahalah*, "inheritance" or "heritage," which suggests something that happened in the remote past in God's plan. So Moses is declaring that long before his day and that of his hearers such a one as Abraham had a meaningful place within God's plan. In that case this noun refers not only to people but also to the land (e.g., Exod. 15:15-17; 2 Sam. 21:3; 1 Kgs. 8:36). In our present age of multitudes of displaced persons, we are shown how deeply important to the human psyche is the issue of our relationship to our environment. And so, as the biblical revelation proceeds, using Moses' Song as a quarry, we are shown that all persons everywhere are in fact displaced persons, for whom God has prepared room to "stand tall" in the kingdom of heaven. Meanwhile God's loving plan for Israel (God's "specimen people" as Lev. 26:12-13 implies) is to give them a special place to live where they may grow in grace and obedience and love of neighbor.

The RSV now makes a deliberate change in the text when, for the Hebrew "children of Israel" (see RSV mg), it reads "sons of God." (The NRSV has only "the number of the gods.") The RSV does so on several bases. First, this change would be in accord with a frequent Ugaritic usage. In the Baal epic the goddess Asherah had seventy sons. Second, it pays attention to this translation in the Dead Sea Scrolls (see Patrick W. Skehan, "A Fragment of the 'Song of Moses' [Deut. 32] from Qumran," 12). Third, this change is found in the LXX, the Greek Version of the OT, which is then followed by the Latin and Syriac Versions of the early Christian period.

We should note that (1) the epic poems of Ugarit, theologically speaking, have no relationship whatsoever with the Song of Moses, and that (2) all the Versions we have named come from a thousand years after the Song was first sung, and share an ideological atmosphere that had been created by the forces of the Hellenistic world. It was the latter that produced the spurious doctrine of guardian angels which in turn presided over the seventy different nations of Gen. 10, as we see at Dan. 10:13, 20, 21; 12:1; Sir. 17:17. These are frequently alluded to in postbiblical Jewish literature, but have no relationship to the Song of Moses in the original Hebrew. The idea would then be, as S. R. Driver writes in his commentary on Deuteronomy, "that the nations were allotted to the care of subordinate divine beings . . . , while Jehovah presided over Israel Himself" (356). Such a misreading of Moses' intention naturally led to the rise of various heretical cults in early NT times. The NJV, however, remains faithful to the Hebrew text.

Yet we have to admit that both readings may be correct at the same time. For the nations, also as peoples of Yahweh, were elect as well as Israel. They were elect, in some cases, to be the agents of the wrath of God against Israel (e.g., Hab. 1:5-11). Yet in so acting they fall victim to that same wrath which they were elected to convey, for not discharging their mission as a divine task. Instead they acted in human pride (Isa. 8:9). Despite their pride, however, all peoples are finally to find salvation (Isa. 2:2-4; 45:23). That is why the nations, along with Israel, are never equated with the kingdom of God, but are always contrasted with it (Dan. 4:34b; Zech. 8:20-23; Isa. 44:5; and finally Matt. 28:19).

Let us quote Walther Eichrodt here (*Theodicy in the OT,* 23). "It is at this point that Israel's faith in the special divine guidance of its history gives rise to the boldest statements. Here a firm bond is established between Israel's fate and that of the rest of mankind, but which the nations, or in the final analysis, their history, can also appear as the object of divine providence."

The fact that the surviving fragment of the Dead Sea Scrolls manuscript reads *beney elohim,* "sons of God," instead of the *beney yisrael* of the MT is no proof that it represents the original Mosaic wording. This is because the whole conception of Israel's election to service as a priest to the nations, as the suffering servant for others, had been gradually dismissed from Israel's consciousness by the time of Ezra and Nehemiah, a couple of hundred years before the formation of the Qumran community. We are aware that at certain points the Scrolls demonstrate more *eisegesis* than *exegesis* of Moses, more interpretation of what the community wanted to find in the biblical text than what was actually there. The Qumran community exemplifies the view held by elements in Judaism which have believed to this day that to be a light to the Gentiles means only to show forth before the eyes of the world an exemplary moral character and, in the modern scene, to be a supporter of all good causes.

The list of the nations of mankind in Gen. 10 numbers seventy (vv. 31-32). In parallel with this we note that the "sons of Israel" who descended into Egypt were also seventy in number (Exod. 1:5), that is, seventy *nephesh* or heads of clans (cf. also Gen. 46:27). It was while they were in Egypt, undergoing the "holocaust" of the Egyptian oppression, that the Israelites were elected by God to be his covenant people (Exod. 19:5). This redeemed people were now the descendants of the original seventy clans. Since the Song of Moses precedes in time both the J and the P narratives of the Pentateuch, the vitality of oral tradition is clearly revealed in this verse. For the Song of Moses must have been passed down in the form of verse for several generations before it could even have met up with the traditions recorded in the J material put together about the time of Solomon.

"According to the number of the sons of God," as the Hebrew text has it, Israel was composed of seventy clans and the Gentiles amounted to seventy nations. It is this equation to which the poem must refer. Here then we have the solution to the choice of terms, "sons of Israel" as against "sons of God," one which depends upon a proper understanding of the doctrine of election.

We noted above that Israel itself persisted in misunderstanding its election. Yet there were always those who rebelled against this "orthodoxy," especially from the time of Deutero-Isaiah and then of Trito-Isaiah (see George A. F. Knight, *Servant Theology* and *The New Israel*). The hard discipline of the Babylonian exile was needed to teach some in Israel that they were elected, not to dominate but to serve. Broken and dispirited on the plains of Babylon, a remnant of Israel listened to the preaching of Deutero-Isaiah and allowed it to change their whole understanding of the significance of the Covenant. The prophet had taught, "You are my *servant*, I have chosen you . . . I will uphold you" (Isa. 41:8-10). Then he went on to say, "I have given you as a covenant to the people, a light to the nations" (42:6) . . . "that my salvation may reach to the end of the earth" (49:6). The prophet was of course referring back to the Mosaic covenant made at Sinai, which was composed in two clauses (Exod. 19:1-5): (1) "You shall be my treasured possession out of all the peoples." This was most heartening to learn, but for what purpose was Israel chosen? (2) "To be a priestly kingdom," holy because God is holy (Lev. 19:2), conveying and mediating God's holy love to his flock, the seventy nations of the world.

Israel's election is thus ultimately bound up with service to the seventy nations, with bringing them the light of God's salvation; and, as Deutero-Isaiah eventually revealed, by going themselves the way of holy, suffering love (Isa. 53).

We might make two more points. When Jesus sent out seventy disciples to preach the good news of the kingdom (Luke 10), surely he saw his act as the outcome of the election of Israel, and so as what the New Covenant was meant to accomplish. The other is an interesting possibility. Since the origin of the name for the Greek translation of the OT — Septuagint, LXX ("Seventy") — is shrouded in myth, might this title not be a deliberate hint on the part of the best minds who made the translation into Greek, that Israel's election must not be confined within bonds as the "beloved" elect of God? Ought it not to be shared with the whole seventy nations of mankind and be given to them in the *koine*, the common language of the Mediterranean and the Near East?

This argument may be seen to be based on the words of Deut. 32:8: "according to the number of the sons of Israel." The tradition remembered (Num. 11:16) that seventy elders ruled over Israel. By NT times the Great Sanhedrin was composed of seventy members plus the chairman. In the following century Josephus, commander in chief in Galilee, appointed seventy elders to rule the territory. The rabbis taught that the Torah had been offered to all the seventy nations of the earth *before* the election of Israel, in seventy languages.

This line of argument leads to the suggestion made above that perhaps both readings "sons of God" and "sons of Israel" may be retained together. Throughout the book of Exodus Israel is known as the "host" (i.e., "army," *tsaba*) of the LORD. But God had his host of "sons" above, also seventy in number. What we have here then might be a pictorial way of declaring that all Israel, God's elect people, was of eschatological significance for the fulfillment of God's cosmic plan; for Yahweh is Judge of all the earth, that is, of all creation (Ps. 94:2). Consequently Ps. 82:6 can say, "I say, 'You are gods, children of the Most High, all of you; nevertheless, you shall die like mortals, and fall like any prince." What unites the gods and mankind is that neither is aware of God's loving plan for them.

Actually the MT never speaks of *beney Yahweh* (sons of Yahweh), only of *beney el* (or *elohim* or *elim*) and so only of gods in general, of whom God was the Father of their divine council. But these were the gods of the seventy nations (cf. Gen. 10:31-32). Israel, on the other hand, was Yahweh's firstborn son in quite another sense, one that was wholly bound up with Israel's election within the plan of God (Exod. 4:22; Deut. 14:1; Isa. 49:6).

The quarrying of Moses' Song reveals the extreme importance of human life that is emphasized when Moses contemplates God's action in uniting himself in covenant with his chosen people. Yahweh is eternal (signified by the pictorial term "Rock"), so the content of his covenant must also be eternal and must affect both realms of matter and spirit at the same time. Admittedly Moses — and most of the OT — seems to have no explicit comprehension of life beyond death, the result of his belief in the unity of all creation. Still mankind is created as one unified personality, "body, soul, and spirit," just as God himself is one and mankind is made in his image. God's covenant love *(hesed)* lasts *le'olam* ("into eternity)", untouched by what we regard as the death of the human person (cf. Ps. 136). This quarrying continues in the theology of Paul, who in 1 Cor. 15 reveals his impatience with his contemporaries who reject the "bodily" resurrection, as do Hinduism and the many modern anthroposophical groups. Many hope to believe that the truth lies with the Eastern teaching of the transmigration of individual naked "souls." Indeed, Paul says in 1 Cor. 15 that God gives the dead believer a "spiritual body" — to complete him as a whole person. That is to say God resurrects, recreating his beloved to be what he or she was in earthly life, yet without sin. So Paul points to the resurrected Christ to demonstrate the oneness of matter and spirit, heaven and earth, body and soul, when sin and evil no longer prevail to divide them. This of course is what Moses taught in his Song — a belief now common to the three monotheistic faiths, Judaism, Christianity, and Islam. It is what eventuates in the NT under the hope for "a new heaven (spirit) and a new earth (matter)" together as one.

v. 9   The LORD's own portion was his people,
        Jacob his allotted heritage.

A number of scholars have dubbed the Song of Moses a *rib* and labelled it "The Lawsuit of God." Such a description might be apt for a sixth-century writing, in that more than one of the great prophets did produce such forms of oratory. But we must dismiss it of Moses, now that we are able to attribute the Song to him without doubt. At any rate it is presumptuous on our part to straightjacket such an ancient poem as this within the bonds of the various classifications of Hebrew literature that moderns have thought up in the light of the literature of later centuries. The poem is not a lawsuit; it is good news about God! The LORD did not choose to work out his plan by means of direct revelation to all the seventy nations. To that end God's "share" (NEB) was Israel, the "heritage" that the Almighty chose to "allot" to himself. In other words, Israel was God's "own possession" (Exod. 19:5; Jer. 10:16).

The word *segullah* ("personal possession"), used at Exod. 19:5 in the giving of the Covenant, would paint a picture in the mind of the ordinary family in Israel in the same manner as did the telling of a parable in NT times. An Eastern king owned everything in his wide dominon, even the goods and chattels in the homes of his subjects. But that could give him little personal satisfaction. So in his palace he kept a box containing his private personal ornaments and jewelry. In this way he found real satisfaction in fingering his treasures as he declared "These are really mine." What a picture of royal fatherly love and care, then, this "parable" offered to Israel.

Yet Yahweh permits the gods of the nations both to exist and to exercise rule. This "permission" is pictured for us in turn by the development of the idea of the heavenly court discussed at Deut. 32:8 (e.g., Jer. 23:18, 22), where each god was assigned his own "seat" by the Judge of all the earth (Ps. 94:2; Deut. 4:19).

Building upon Moses' "parable," then, Deutero-Isaiah continued to declare that God not only loved his own special people (Isa. 43:4), he was actually to be found *in* (Heb. *be*) Israel, in that he was hidden in his covenant relationship with them (Isa. 45:14-15). The KJV translates correctly here: "Surely God is in thee." Thus, since God's purpose was that all peoples should come to know and confess him as LORD (Isa. 45:23), Israel was not chosen just to be God's favorite people. Israel was chosen for a purpose. God's covenantal presence *in* Israel empowered Israel to be his servant for the task of bringing all the nations of the earth to salvation through suffering love.

We are bound to recognize that much which the NT has to say about Christians being "called" *(kletoi)* "according to his purpose" (Rom. 1:6; 1 Cor. 1:24; Jude 1) stems back to this statement in the Song of Moses. Yet Paul must also show that Christians are no saints *(hagioi)* by nature, but only because they have been called in mission to the seventy races of humanity, through grace, by a prevenient act of God in Christ. (We note that Israel is not one of the seventy races listed in Gen. 10, for Israel is unique). This explanation by Paul of the meaning of election was needed in his day since, according to the several Targums on Isa. 40–66, all Israel was not prepared to think in terms of election to service. We note then that Moses' "Word" here negates the doctrine of double election that has plagued the Christian church all down the centuries.

v. 10   He found him in a desert land,
        in a howling wilderness waste;
    he shielded him, cared for him,
        guarded him as the apple of his eye.

What a picture of prevenient grace this is! Nowhere in the Bible do we find what the world's religions and ideologies are primarily concerned with — the search for God by mankind. What we read, in this important "quarry" for a construction of the biblical revelation, is "He (Yahweh) found him" (RSV; NRSV "sustained"). So we discover that what God "found" was a "foundling." This reality that it was God who found mankind and not mankind who found "God" as in the Greek myths and in the modern world religions, is maintained within the theology of the Old and the New Covenants right throughout both Testaments. As Abraham Heschel declares in *The Prophets:* "Israel's faith is not the fruit of a quest for God. Israel did not discover God. The Bible is the record of God's approach to man" (439). The Targums emphasize this by substituting "his Shekhinah" for "he," meaning God's localized presence, the emphasis therefore being on "his loving care."

While of course the wilderness of Sinai looks to be the geographical and historical reference behind "in a desert land," we should not expect the poem to be taken literally, for Moses is speaking theologically. We are to understand the desert over against the theological reality that God does not create ex nihilo per se; rather he creates out of chaos (Gen. 1:2). Chaos is the word *tohu* that is found here in parallel with desert, a word which is emphasized at Isa. 43:19. "Wilderness" was thus the first "place," though it was no place, just perhaps non-sacred space (cf. Jer. 4:23), variously described as the "place" of "howling," of burning thirst, and of a dried up landscape. One of the Targums describes the wilderness as the abode of demons, which identified themselves to mankind in the form of serpents. That is why the taking up of serpents means to control the demons within them (see Deut. 32:24, where Moses returns to this theme). Isaiah 43:19-20 later spiritualizes the "wilderness."

Thus the wilderness is as much a picture of life in Egypt before the Exodus as is the Sinai desert, for that life was indeed a moral chaos. Thus it was "out of Egypt" that God called his son (Hos. 11:1), although the same prophet spoke of returning to the wilderness (Hos. 2:14), there to "honeymoon" with God. We note incidentally that Jesus describes basic human nature before its redemption especially as revealed in vv. 15-17 to follow. Between Moses and Jesus, Ezek. 16:3 had interpreted this verse to show that "chaos" is found not only in nature but also in the civilizations of mankind: "Your origin and your birth were in the land of the Canaanites; your father was an Amorite, and your mother a Hittite." Ezekiel then proceeds to describe the baby as an unwanted abortion.

It is unfortunate that the NJB translates all the verbs in this section as if, grammatically, they were imperfects and so employs the present tense in English. The result is to suggest that God keeps on rescuing Israel throughout its history. This interpretation seems to suggest a dogmatic reading into the text of what it is not saying.

William F. Albright, putting the idea of the foundling and of chaos together, suggests that in the light of the language of the contemporary Babylonian and Hittite laws the verb *matsah*, "found," can be understood to mean "caught," as if God were grasping to rescue the child from the powers of evil.

Now there follows a series of verbs which emphasize just this point. The verb behind NRSV "shielded" means to surround on all sides (RSV "encircled"), as if to show there can be no escape from the encircling arms of God's love. "Cared for" is a verb expressing mental and moral purpose. It is a polel form in Hebrew, signifying "turning the mind to give one's whole attention to." These words offer in part a description of the giving of the Covenant at Exod. 19:1-5. Thus we recognize the mighty power of concern that these verbs convey. They reveal that Almighty God is giving his whole attention to this "baby," this foundling, this child who was suffering the horrors of *yeshimon*, this non-being of chaos.

Ezekiel 16 quoted above adds much color to this verse (Ezek. 16:1-6). This foundling was an unwanted abortion ("one untimely born," i.e., "born out of due time," as Paul referred it to himself in continuity with this passage; 1 Cor. 15:8). Its "navel cord was not cut," its little body was not washed, nor was it "rubbed with salt, nor wrapped in cloths." Rather, it was "thrown out in the open field, . . . abhorred on the day you were born," a "barbarian," a foreigner, an obnoxious parody of a human child.

The contrast between human care, even natural mother love, and the total care of Yahweh for this repugnant aborted baby is vividly expressed in the next phrase, he "guarded him as the apple of his eye" (cf. Ps. 17:8). Our English idiom derives from this verse, but is not as expressive as the Hebrew. Actually what Yahweh guarded, preserved, and lovingly looked after was a dear little person — a wee human being — for that is what the Hebrew means, with reference to the tiny reflexion of a person in another's eye. This then is no picture of natural mother love, especially if the mother has aborted and abandoned her baby. It gives us a vivid insight into the biblical term "grace," for it shows us what love for the unlovable entails.

Moses emphasizes this gracious act of God by employing a number of verbs in this passage — e.g., elect, single out, accept, embrace, call. These verbs all speak of acts of sheer grace, such as were surely not invented centuries later, presumably in Josiah's day.

Some in our modern society ask why there is no phrase in the Apostles' Creed such as "God is love," since such is the central tenet of our faith. But it is the OT which actually lets us "see" God acting his love toward the people whom he had chosen to be the servant of his kingdom (cf. Ps. 136). The OT lets us discover that love is not a sentiment but an activity, and as such the concept of love can hardly be expressed in our Creed.

Thus it is that God's love for us shows how God sees us. A husband can still see in his wife, now old and pained with arthritis, the one with whom he has shared an exciting life together, ever since he fell in love with her when she was a girl ("the wife of his youth"). That is, there is a revelation here of the "faith" that God had in this foundling when he set his love upon him, faith that some day this Israel, despite its inevitable rebellion, would eventually become God's chosen instrument for the building of his kingdom among all nations.

Those NT scholars who have sought to demonstrate that it is impossible to discover the "historical Jesus" have been blind to the revelation of the "historical God" in the OT. The God of Moses is the same God as the God of the NT, and the Father of the "historical Jesus." As Albright says in more than one of his works, "The NT was intended as a supplement to the OT and not a replacement."

This foundling then became the adopted son of God, as Israel is called at Exod. 4:22. In his commentary on Colossians (Minneapolis: Augsburg, 1982), Eduard Schweizer has pointed out that "son" had become a comparatively common term for Israel before the development of Christianity; for example, he writes (*The Letter to the Colossians*, 35), it is to be found in Ps. Sol. 17–18; Jub. 1:24-25; 4QFlor 1:7-8; and 4QDibHam 3:4-8. Since the NT regards Jesus as the epitome of Israel, it is easy to see how the epithet "son" was applied to him, and why Jesus was regarded as the "end product" of God's "faith" in the foundling's future as the chosen instrument in God's plan. Not only so, but since the "teaching" (Deut. 32:2) of Moses is not at all what we like to delineate as "spiritual," but is rather highly materialistic, it forms the bridge that links the two sons in this act of God's love.

The modern day atheist's concept of love is purely humanistic, based on what he or she has humanly conceived love to be — a misapprehension that has now clouded out any idea of the existence of God. Although one often hears that "Christianity means loving your neighbor," actually it does not. Together with Judaism Christianity places first the *command* of God at Deut. 6:4: "Hear, O Israel: the LORD is our God, the LORD alone. You shall love the LORD your God with all your heart, and with all your soul, and with all your might." Love for others and for self only follow from obedience to the great command. This is because loving the God whose actions Moses describes in his Song links one with what divine love is really like, which is unspeakably far from what human beings believe love to be. No

49

human could ever have invented the concept that the God of Israel *is* love in Moses' sense.

v. 11 As an eagle stirs up its nest
and hovers over its young;
as it spreads its wings, takes them up,
and bears them aloft on its pinions,

"As an eagle" makes a direct reference to the preamble leading to the giving of the Covenant (Exod. 19:4). Sinai is composed of a high, rocky, barren series of peaks. Eagles (or here, the griffon vulture) have at all times made their homes and built their nests near the tops of high precipices. There they bring up their young. These are fed by their parents until their wings can support them in the air. When father eagle believes his eaglets are developed enough to fly alone, he pushes them out of the nest. They might well plummet to their death if they are not yet able to control their wings. If such is the case, father eagle (the Hebrew term could imply either sex) flies down quicker than the baby eagle's fall, goes beneath it, stretches out his wings, and lets the baby eaglet fall upon his back. Then father eagle flies back up to the eyrie and deposits his little one once again in the nest. He then waits some days, perhaps until he believes his young eaglet will be able to fly this time on its own, having now developed the power of its wings sufficiently to become independent. Whether this is a scientifically accurate picture of a father eagle's activities I am not sure; but it is what was thought in the ancient world when people were not easily able to observe the ways of the eagle as they gazed upwards from the bottom of a precipice.

Jesus adapts this picture for the understanding of city dwellers by speaking of his own loving care for the people of Jerusalem in terms of a mother hen and her chicks (Matt. 23:37). The basic significance, however, is the occurrence of the root *rahaph*, rendered here by "hovers over." This is the verb used of the action of the Spirit of God at Gen. 1:2. There the Spirit "sweeps" or "moves over" the face of the waters of chaos. In like manner we are told that the nature of the adopted son is indeed chaotic until such time as the Father's loving care can woo him to respond to his love by showing in his turn a measure of love and obedience.

"Taking them up" is translated warmly in the LXX by *dechesthai*. Particularly with the addition of the prefix *eis* this verb is employed in the LXX of receiving someone into a circle of fellowship. It was thus that Jesus "received" sinners (Luke 15:2), even as we find the word used at Ezek. 20:41. On the one hand the Greek translators could see in this picture the eagle waiting to ensure its young one was indeed autonomous before swooping into Egypt to its aid (sic!), and then picking Israel up out of that land of "chaos." On the other hand they could not envisage how the eagle could *ya'ir* ("stir up") its babes as an act of education; so they translate simply by "watch over" *(skepazo)*, losing the deep awareness of the Hebrew verb.

Besides the verb *rahaph*, which links Moses with Jesus, there is another word which links Genesis with Jesus: *gozelim*. This is what the young eaglets are called in this verse. The term denotes robbers, despoilers, destructive creatures, because of course they were raptors, birds of prey — no innocent babes such as the LXX likes to assume by its use of Gk. *nossia*, meaning brood or nest. The wilderness *(midbar)* was not just a picture, a symbol of chaos and evil, as we have seen it to be. It was also a refuge for outlaws and fugitives (Gen. 21:14). So this was no innocent blue-eyed boy that Yahweh had adopted. Israel was the unwanted cast-off of a brigand encampment who was already showing signs of his rapacious background.

Again it is appropriate to cite B. F. Westcott, the great NT scholar of the nineteenth century: "No fact, I think, is sadder in the history of religious thought than that Augustine had no real knowledge of Greek" (cited by W. Robertson Nicoll, *Princes of the Church*, 145) — and even less of Hebrew. Yet so much of orthodoxy has been dependent upon Augustine right up until the rise of the study of OT theology in the past hundred years. For example, the concept exhibited by the postbiblical Hebrew term *shekinah,* meaning the "overdwelling" of God in his love upon his beloved, has had to be learned from the Christian study of Jewish theology. It is built from the root *sh-k-n,* "to dwell," for its significance is pictured in terms of Moses' eagle as it hovers with outstretched wings over Israel in love and remaining thus to "rest" with God's people. Moreover, it has been noted only in the last century that John's Gospel employs the Greek root *skenoo,* whose consonants are identical with the Hebrew term, to declare that "the Word became flesh and *dwelt* among us, full of grace and truth" (John 1:14 RSV).

God's action in snatching the child Israel (cf. Hos. 11:1) out of the "howling wilderness" (paralleling thereby the work of the Spirit in Gen. 1:1-3) is what later OT writers saw to be one of his "mighty acts," a *geburah,* a *dynamis.* These terms reveal that the Holy Spirit is known by its action to be love, even as Yahweh himself is love (cf. Ps. 136). To a bystander what happened to Israel in Egypt and in the wilderness would appear as just a series of natural events. But the Holy Spirit enlightened Moses' mind to see these events *sub specie aeternitatis,* as acts of God each with its own eschatological significance. Similarly in the NT we read at Matt. 11:20, "He began to reproach the cities in which most of his 'mighty works' had been done, because they did not repent," that is, they were not willing to acknowledge God's redeeming love in action in these works.

In this way, then, the Song of Moses describes the first phase of the covenantal relationship between God and Israel, expressed in terms of a drama. "It is the thorny, conflicted, seductive, unpredictable unfolding epic of a covenant relationship between Yahweh and Adam, Yahweh and Abraham, Yahweh and Israel, Yahweh and humanity" (Thomas C. Oden, *The Living God,* 233). It is the "first phase" only, on the grounds of Moses' deep awareness that God is both the living God (Deut. 32:40) and the God of love (v. 36). Therefore even as God endures forever, so will his covenant love. Nor is the drama only about

52

Israel per se, as if Israel were an autonomous, independent entity within creation, about whom one could write "The History of Israel." Israel, without the grace of God, would be a mere "nothing," an unwanted foundling (Ezek. 16:4-5), until *God* "said" to Israel, "Live! and grow up" (vv. 6-7). Only then did the foundling come to life.

> vv. 12-13   The LORD alone guided him,
> no foreign god was with him.
> He set him atop the heights of the land,
> and fed him with produce of the field;
> he nursed him with honey from the crags,
> with oil from flinty rock.

This exultant couple of verses point to the wonder that only Yahweh of all the gods of mankind (cf. Isa. 43:11-12; Hos. 13:4), and of all the religions of the world — including those that have persisted to this day — could have adopted and actually did adopt a repulsive and vicious child and then "led" him *(nahah)*, in the sense that a shepherd guards and leads his sheep (Ps. 103:4-5; 136). Deuteronomy 31:8 interprets v. 12 ("The LORD alone guided him"): going before you, being with you, not failing nor forsaking you (cf. Exod. 3:12). The depth of biblical love is the greatest of all mysteries (Deut. 1:31). From what Moses says here, we too can discover that if we but allow God to *lead* us, then our activities become genuine; moreover, we are then able to transform nature to serve humanity, to produce food from the soil, and to enjoy "the blood of the grape" in true fellowship.

The biblical tradition is so very different from the religions of humanity that it cannot be regarded as merely one of a number or as aspects of universal truth. The biblical faith, for example, cannot be regarded as the fulfillment of the Hindu view of personality, though the Hindu traditions are as ancient as Moses. The knowledge of God as Truth is something that comes only by being practiced, lived out in history, and not reached by reason or mere human intelligence.

Wonder passes over into ecstasy. Riding on the high places of the earth is a common biblical picture of such ecstasy (cf. Ps. 18:33 = 2 Sam. 22:34). The rider can be likened to a stag or a deer that leaps lightly and lightheartedly from mountaintop to mountaintop (cf. Hab. 3:17-19, where we have exultation in the face of total disaster). Our modern phrase might be "I am up in the clouds, on cloud nine." The text refers to the experience of receiving a gift from God, the gift of total forgiveness and so of grace bestowed. No wonder that leads to a joy that is not of this world.

But now we are to note the extreme paradox that it was upon *gozelim* that this grace was bestowed, for we saw at Deut. 32:11 that this noun means destructive, malicious, rapacious youth!

God's grace is pictured for us, not as it is in itself, but only as it can be grasped and understood by the itinerant folk of Moses' day. To eat the produce of the "field" (better, "common grazing ground") was possible only on attainment of the Promised Land they had not yet reached. Was Moses speaking of the eschatological hope, as we might do, and as Israel certainly did at Isa. 27:6? And as Ezekiel did when he shared with his people the trauma of life in the "wilderness" of Babylon so many centuries later (Ezek. 36:30)?

To suck honey from the rock is to suck from the breasts of Mother Earth (cf. Isa. 66:11). The verb infers smacking the lips and saying, "How good and kind God is." Olive trees that give oil can grow in rocky ground ("flinty rock") otherwise uncultivable by humans — and so we have a glimpse of a miracle of grace. For example, at Deut. 8:15 we are told that it was God, there described as Rock, who gave Israel water out of the flinty rock. What we have here, though, are words of encouragement given to God's beloved to have them prepare for a banquet out of the resources of the earth, a joyous occasion, one that will be provided by God. In this way the common act of eating together *may,* if God so wills, take on eschatological significance and become a sacramental act of communion between God and mankind. The grace of God then invades Israel, sinful Israel, leading them to share in his joy (Isa. 25:6-9). Thus God makes Israel "ride high" in the ecstasy of fellowship with God.

Unlike a century ago, we have virtually absolute agreement on the historicity of the person Moses, even though his activities seem to be remembered only in terms of saga. No evidence has been found to trace Israel's route from Mt. Sinai through the wilderness, and any efforts by the authors of the Pentateuch to map those journeys would only have amounted to a false attempt at historicizing Moses and his people. Nevertheless, archaeological and literary evidence does seem to underscore the basic social and cultural phenomena recorded. For example, Israeli engineers have unearthed a range of underground reservoirs in the Negeb (cf. Josh. 15:19), such as may have been available to the nomadic peoples of Moses' time, suggesting that the "wilderness" was not so bleak then as it is today.

In Deut. 32:13 we have also a picture of the orderliness of nature, of the round of the seasons, of the interdependence of bees, cows, lambs, and rams, wheat and the vine, upon each other and upon the sunshine and the rain — in other words of God's "providence," of God's "upholding" all his creatures in time and space in an ordered existence (Ps. 104:5-23). And all this for a foundling child, who as we read at Deut. 32:15 "grew fat" from the good food of the land, and "kicked." Yet God, being God, never swerves from what he has done once, and will do again, and yet again. Recalling this verse the prophet Deutero-Isaiah, in the "wilderness" of the Exile, assures his people that God will forgive, renew, and "feed" them once again as he had already done in Moses' day (Isa. 43:20).

There is a strongly visual image here of the relationship between the action of God towards a human being and God's action through that person. Such an action of "the Spirit of the LORD" is described at Judg. 6:34. There the NRSV reads: "The Spirit of the LORD took possession of Gideon" — surely a weak rendering of the Hebrew, which reads "The Spirit of the LORD put on Gideon as his clothing." So it is with the love of God. Humans are not able to love their neighbor in the deep sense of the word known only within the Covenant; Westerners, for example, confuse it with liking another person, with mother love, or with sexual attraction — until God has put his love upon a person as if it were clothing. Then, and only then, can one "love his neighbor as himself."

> v. 14   Curds from the herd, and milk from the flock,
>   with fat of lambs and rams;
>   Bashan bulls and goats,
>   together with the choicest wheat —
>   you drank fine wine from the blood of grapes.

This verse continues to list the gracious gifts of God that could be used to prepare the banquet. This figure of a banquet is of course employed throughout both Testaments to help us poor mortal creatures merely begin to grasp the wonder and joy of fellowship with the eternal God, and with one another through him (Isa. 58:14; Ps. 81:16; Luke 22:14-19, 30). It is the NEB that perhaps gives the clearest rendering of this verse. "Curds" was something like our yogurt. "Bashan" cows, like our "Jersey" or "Hereford" varieties, were fed on the best-watered area of Palestine, to the east of the river Jordan. The fat of lamb's kidneys, being the best of the meat, was normally dedicated to go up in smoke in a sacrificial act. This showed something of the nature of the banquet with mankind sharing in God's portion.

The components of the banquet have all already been provided by God. The orderly providence of God, mediated through his covenant with Noah (Gen. 8) and made evident through the sequence of day and night, sunshine and shower, summer and winter, lies behind the whole concept of Palestine being a land of milk and honey. Moses is aware that God has a relationship not only with his people by covenant, but also by covenant with all his own complex creation. We recall the enthusiastic report about the riches of the land that the spies whom Moses sent on ahead brought back to their desert headquarters (Num. 13).

There sounds what is almost an eschatologically significant hint in the last words of Deut. 32:14: "*you* drank fine wine from the blood of grapes," as today we think of its relevance to holy communion. The word here is *hemer*, not *yayin*, the ordinary word for wine. *Hemer* is rather bubbling wine like champagne. Then again, the sudden change from the third to the second person *you* is surely a kind of *argumentum ad hominem*. It is employed in the same sense as the barb which Nathan shot at King David: "*You* are the man" (2 Sam. 12:7). All this stems back to what we read at Exod. 18:9: "Jethro rejoiced for all the good that the LORD had done to Israel."

We can well understand that the Israelites had by now reached the land of Moab, an area that was quite well watered and moderately rich in natural resources. Since this was where Moses was soon to die, he had by now been given firsthand knowledge of what the Promised Land was like (Deut. 34).

v. 15   Jacob ate his fill;
      Jeshurun grew fat, and kicked.
      You grew fat, bloated, and gorged!
    He abandoned God who made him,
    and scoffed at the Rock of his salvation.

In what reads like an almost insouciant sequence we meet now with the enormity of Israel's ingratitude. In this case it shows itself as total disobedience, the bitter sin of one who rebels against the bonds of a covenant. And it stems from pride, that sin which we today regard as the first of the Seven Deadly Sins.

The name "Jeshurun" here given to Israel seems to be a kind of "pet" name given lovingly to a well-beloved and only child.

To the eye in Hebrew it looks like the name Israel. It may possibly derive from the word *yashar,* meaning "upright," but used here of course in irony. It occurs also twice in the following chapter, Deut. 33 (at vv. 5 and 26), clearly a very ancient poem. Isaiah 44:2 takes it from here centuries later in order to rediscover for exiled Israel the love and care of God for the people whom he was even then chastising (see George A. F. Knight, *Servant Theology,* 75-76).

The LXX does not understand this nuance of love for the fallen. It gets rid of this pet name and translates merely by adding a line, not found in the Hebrew, in which it refers only to "Jacob." John Calvin, living long before the era of critical studies, put his finger on the issue by saying, "This is the ideal name for Israel, showing how far they had defected."

The word "kicked" *(ba'at)* is evidently an early term also, as it occurs only once again, and in an early book, at 1 Sam. 2:29. The picture is of a domestic animal, perhaps a cow that had been well treated and well fed, now grown fat, thick and sleek, turning around and giving its owner a vicious kick. A cow is domesticated to be of use to its master, not to kick. So with the adopted and now adolescent son. "He abandoned God who made him" to be what he was meant to be — a handsome youth, and very different from the ugly castaway foundling he had been. He did so, not by demanding his birthright as in the story of the Prodigal Son and then just leaving home. Rather, he kicked his father and scoffed at him, meaning in the Hebrew calling his own father a fool and sneering that the "salvation" he had experienced was mere nonsense. Sin is a living activity. To use a modern expression, what he did was to kick his father "in the teeth," through which the words of adoptive love had issued to reach forth to his heart. Human beings seem to be quite as enthusiastic about living in disobedience as in obedience (cf. Ps. 95:8-11). Some scholars suggest that *Jeshurun* comes from *shor,* an ox, because such a beast might be expected to kick!

But there is more to "grew fat" than this. Israel was to

become fat at the expense of a depressed Canaanite peasantry. They had already shown signs of such egotism before the eyes of Moses (Exod. 16:3). As a result of breaking the First Commandment of obedience and loyalty to the God of love, love for one's neighbor was dismissed as merely stupid. In the Book of the Covenant (Exod. 20–23) as much concern is expressed for the need to love and care for the poor and needy as to obey the Word of God. Consequently the great prophets can build upon this passage again and again. For example, Amos can call the rich "ladies" of Samaria "fat cows," for they "oppress the poor" and "crush the needy" (Amos 4:1), and he can denounce the rich merchants who "trample on the needy, and bring to ruin the poor of the land" (8:4). So in general Robert Gordis can say it describes religious insensibility (*The Book of Job* [New York: Ktav, 1978], 164). We are faced with the reality that, to this day, in any "land of milk and honey" people tend to neglect spiritual values and to put their trust rather in what money can buy.

Another mark of the ancientness of the Song is that where the early name for Israel, Jeshurun, occurs there also appears the early name for God, *eloah* and not *elohim*. Consequently when Habakkuk chooses language taken from the Song he declares, "*Eloah* came from Teman," with reference to the life of Moses (Hab. 3:3).

In a number of later OT passages the call to obedience is sometimes made *in order that* one might be saved. But in the Song of Moses (as in the Song of the Lamb, Rev. 15:3), the call to obedience is made because one has already been saved and created anew. Thus our Song shows that salvation is not something that we can just "possess," or simply have at our disposal. Such a theology also points to the antiquity of the Song, in that it was sung in light of God's act in saving his people from slavery in Egypt.

In fact, we "possess" nothing. Jeshurun's "fall" was inevitable, in that evil existed before "the" fall (Gen. 1:2; 3:22). Jeshurun merely inherited the fate of humanity. As part of mankind

Israel could not, of his own volition and in his own strength, turn and walk back into the garden to regain the life intended for him from the tree of life (Gen. 3:24). Only God can rescue Israel from his fate, certainly not any of the "new gods" whom he decides to worship (Deut. 32:17). Or to quote Augustine (d. A.D. 430), "Original sin means only sin at the origin, answered by forgiveness at the climax." God is "the Rock, his work is perfect" (v. 4). Therefore God knew from the "origin" that Israel would "grow fat and kick," even as he "shielded him and cared for him" in the wilderness. But knowing as much does not mean that God foredoomed Israel to rebel. Israel's rebellion in his free will so to do was what God freely knew Israel would do. Israel's act in free will actually serves to emphasize still further the unspeakable grace of God, for human freedom is grounded in, permitted by, and derived from the power of God who is love. "Nothing is too hard (Heb. "wonderful") for the LORD" (Gen. 17:15-17; 18:12-15; Jer. 32:17; Matt. 19:26). "Nothing that God conceives to do and wills to do is beyond God's ability or power to accomplish" (Calvin *Institutes* ii.7.5); this reality the psalmists learned from Moses. Israel's "rebellion" happens over and over again throughout its history (e.g., Isa. 1:2). Thus Paul is by no means the original author of the picture. To sum it up in the words of a modern writer, "Atheists, agnostics, and secularists" reject the Church (as the covenant people) "on grounds that the church *coram Deo* dare not take seriously; Israel rejects the church on grounds that the church *coram Deo* dare not ignore" (Paul M. van Buren, *A Christian Theology of the People Israel,* 2:33).

Paul has the last word, expressing thereby the ultimate result of quarrying from Moses' Song. At 1 Cor. 10:1-3 he writes, "I do not want you to be unaware, brothers and sisters, that our ancestors were all under the cloud" (as Paul's contemporaries had learned, or ought to have, as a result of its having been passed down from generation to generation, as Moses had commanded at Deut. 32:7), "and all passed through the sea, and all were baptized into ('under the hand of') Moses in the cloud and in the sea, and all drank . . . from the spiritual rock . . . and the rock was Christ." The Rock, as we saw at Deut. 32:4, pictorializes the unfailing faithfulness, grace, and steadfast love (*hesed*) of the God of the Covenant, the God whom Paul declares at 2 Cor. 5:19 finally and wholly revealed himself "in Christ." Paul believed then that it was the objectionable infant foundling who was "baptized" in Moses' day, when God took up this baby, "encircled" him, and (as we saw at Deut. 32:10) "turned his mind to give his whole loving self" to the infant. God then named him Jeshurun, his beloved little one. Moreover, that was *as soon as* God found Israel in the howling waste of the wilderness, the realm of sin and chaos (*tohu*), and *before* Jeshurun could scoff at the Rock of his salvation (v. 15). So Moses and Paul together have provided the Church catholic with the theological content to the continuing ecumenical practice of infant baptism.

Moses addresses his people here with an eye to the future, as we can recognize from his use of the second person of the verb. "Jeshurun grew fat, and kicked" is a statement of fact expressed in the third person. But then follows, "*You* grew fat, bloated." "You" is the second person, and so is actually the hearer of the Song. This came about while the Song was still rehearsed in the ears of the following generations. But the "you" becomes "you and me" of the people of God at all times once the Song was preserved in writing. It was then read out in synagogue or church or came home to us as we read it in the privacy of our home. Moses' Song conveys the Word of the Living God; thus it must be as alive today as it sounded in the ears of Joshua and his generation.

vv. 16-17   They made him jealous with strange gods,
      with abhorrent things they provoked him.
They sacrificed to demons, not God,
      to deities they had never known,
to new ones recently arrived,
      whom your ancestors had not feared.

As the years pass, evil indulged in grows in strength and power even as humans grow to be ever more clever (cf. Gen. 4). Today sophisticated humanity sacrifices the poor of a nation to find the means to create nuclear weapons — "demons, not God," gods that previous generations "had never known." In Moses' day, as leader of his people our poet had marched through the homelands of the nations in what is today called Transjordan. Thus he had seen for himself what the gods of Midian, Ammon, and Moab were really like. Later writers spoke of them as "abominations." Their worship included ritual sexual intercourse, ritual murder, along with incest and human sacrifice. It was when Israel chose as its "rock" that which was not the Rock that the collapse of its moral and political cohesion came about (cf. Exod. 32). This collapse is apparent as early as the events recorded in the book of Judges, and very much more by the period of the eighth-century prophets and later still of Jeremiah. Hosea, Isaiah, Ezekiel, Nehemiah, and many Psalms build their case using Moses' language here.

These then were new gods, like our modern new gods nationalism, militarism, consumerism, and technology. To show that they were not divine as was Yahweh, these deities are declared not to be *eloah*, "divinity" as such. The LXX is careful to translate Heb. *hadashim* ("new") by the adjective *kainos*. They were not *neos* (also meaning "new") in the sense of being utterly different, newborn divine beings. They were the old gods that had seduced mankind, only now they were taking on new and fresh forms. As Thomas F. Torrance puts it (*The Apocalypse Today*, 116), "A person can't juggle with stocks and shares [and] be utterly faithful to Christian principles . . . The fact is this, that the whole of our life has become so entangled with economic evil that no one can escape from it."

We note Moses' insistence that *all* Israel had now turned to their new gods, so that *all* Israel was now under God's judgment. Torrance adds that while it is true that we are all tainted by economic evil, we are not called upon to worship it! This is because the moment we do so it becomes an idol.

"You have learned to outdo your ancestors, just in the space of forty years," says Moses; "they had never dreaded such newfangled gods as you have adopted when you crossed through Transjordan, and now your life is ruled by fear." With this last word, "fear" *(se'ar)*, we meet with a double entendre, for the word can mean one or both of two things at once. (1) It can describe the hair of one's head rising in fright. (2) With a change of one vowel (not of course original to the Hebrew) it can mean "demons." Or (3) it can mean both at once, since it may originate in hairy "goat-demons," to which sacrifice was made in orgies (Lev. 17:7). We are reminded of the legend of Frankenstein. Mankind has the power to conjure up gods who then take over control of one's life and who then fill one's soul with horror. But as we have said, these gods are not "new." What we meet with here is the principle of the German philosopher Ludwig Feuerbach, "Mankind creates its gods in its own image." Jesus clearly showed he was "of God" when he sought for fellowship with God in the wilderness among the demons (Mark 1:35), for it was there mankind needed God most.

Once again now, as at Deut. 32:14 and 15, we are presented with the *argumentum ad hominem*. Until now these verses have been about "they"; all at once now Moses speaks of "your" ancestors, pointing his finger at his own contemporaries. This is why some scholars have regarded the Song of Moses as a lawsuit (see above on v. 9). Moses employs an Akkadian term from the rich literature of the coast of Tyre and Sidon, *shedim* ("demons"). Educated at the Egyptian court he had learned how to conduct affairs with envoys from foreign lands, even from as far away as Mesopotamia. He had studied something of their various languages and cultures. Thus Moses would be acquainted with the literature, the epic poems, of the peoples in between.

The worship of the *shedim* was something like how the Chinese trace the signs of the zodiac in acts of worship. In the old days the Chinese peasant simply accepted the revelation and bowed down. It is horrifying to discover that some Israelites in later centuries actually sacrificed their own children to the *shedim* (Ps. 106:37; cf. Deut. 12:31). This was surely both a "hair-raising," and a "demonic" experience (cf. Walter Eichrodt, *Theology of the OT,* 2:224).

Yet, as some suggest, the noun *shedim* may derive from the root *shadad,* "to ruin," "to devastate," to turn what is good into the realm of negation, into the devastation of that chaos which has been the enemy of God's creative purpose from the beginning. Truly Israel must be taught that it lives on the knife-edge between good and evil. At Job 15:20-24, a passage that is dependent upon Moses' Song, Eliphaz describes in awesome terms what results in the soul of the wicked. He descends into darkness, knowing moreover that he is fated to do so — in fact, that he is "destined for the sword." Moses says as much quite clearly at Deut. 32:25.

One more point to note from these verses is that idolatry derived from the worship of gods of another land, with which the god is closely related (cf. v. 8), is sin against the land, the soil of Mother Earth; for it was the LORD who gave all nations their land as their own heritage. This is a firmly held belief by many peoples who are unaffected by Western individualism. They are glad to find at Lev. 25:23 that the LORD declares, "The land is mine." It cannot be sold to a foreigner, and it must not be ill-treated. Those who dwell on it have been placed there by God and are thus to regard it as a "loan." Its produce comes forth from it for them to enjoy. This view becomes incarnated in the Mosaic understanding of the divine plan to settle Israel in the Promised Land.

> v. 18   You were unmindful of the Rock that bore you;
> you forgot the God who gave you birth.

The poignancy of the situation is then expressed in language that has been employed already to reveal God's love and faithfulness. "He (Yahweh) remembered the days of old, of Moses his servant . . ." (Isa. 63:11-14). But Israel did not remember. Moses' indictment continues, "You (not 'they'!) were unmindful of the Rock that bore you" — you, Israel, the firstborn son of God (Exod. 4:22; Isa. 1:2; cf. 17:10), even predestined to be so (Isa. 51:16). Yet God, as Rock, does not change. The fact that God never lets his people go, even when they desert him, is revealed in his unique relationship to them in covenant. Even when in exile *from* Yahweh the prophet Deutero-Isaiah, who was of Israel himself and *with* Israel in Babylon, could have the Gentiles declare, "God is '*in*' you alone. . . .Truly, you are a God who hides himself" (Isa. 45:14-15) — hides *in* a recalcitrant people! No wonder Moses knew his God as Rock. Thomas C. Oden (*The Living God*, 80) writes, "It is nothing short of astonishing to many biblical writers that the all-powerful God paradoxically sustains in being those creatures that oppose God's authority and goodness!"

On the one hand both lines of this verse warn us not to limit God's parenthood of Israel to the word "father." First, emphasis is made that God is *el*, the "divine being," utterly other than ideas of human male and female. The title stands in contrast with the other names used in the Song, Yahweh, Elohim, and Eloah. Yet what we are told is that this *el* writhed in pain at *your* birth, pain such as only a mother can experience. And so the Lord GOD is the one who knows the meaning of pain, the pain inherent in re-creation.

The father-mother parallel is of course picked up from here by later writers, for example at Isa. 45:10; 51:2; Jer. 2:27; 31:20; Prov. 8:24-25; Job 38:28-29; Gal. 4:19. Also Isa. 63:15 can speak of "the trembling of thy womb" (Phyllis Trible, *God and the Rhetoric of Sexuality*).

On the other hand one result of this "unmindfulness" and "forgetting" has been the unbiblical idea that an anthropomorphism is literally true. On the contrary, as the OT proceeds we discover that God never ceases to look upon Israel as "she," unfaithful as "she" is (as his bride), even as his wife (cf. Hos. 1–3; Isa. 50:1; Jer. 31:4, 21, 32). We are aware of a growing use of the name "Zion" for Israel throughout the OT, or even of "Jerusalem." Since cities are feminine in Hebrew, Israel could thus be referred to or addressed in the feminine in Hebrew. Consequently she is "Jerusalem, our mother" (Gal. 4:26).

It is true that while one or two female or motherly elements do actually reveal their presence in the person of the Godhead, Moses only mentions these in passing as mere anthropomorphisms. Having learned the essential "name" directly from God himself to be "I AM" (Exod. 3:14; Deut. 32:39), just as later in the case of Jesus Moses recognized that God's person cannot be described by us creatures of limited insight and of a sexual nature by our categories of being (cf. John 4:24). God's being is beyond all our human categories (Job 38–39; Isa. 55:8-9).

This is not the case with our human institutions, where the elements of male and female naturally enter into our human vocabularies. In the OT the people of God are at times called both son of God and bride or wife of God. In the latter case they are known as God's *'edah,* a word translated in the LXX by *synagoge,* both of which are feminine. The book of Hosea uses both figures of son and wife in parallel. At Jer. 31:32 God declares that he is Israel's husband (cf. also Isa. 50:1). Then he says, "I will build you, and you shall be built" (Jer. 31:4). We note that the word *banah* bears the double meaning of building a house and building a family by begetting children (cf. 2 Sam. 7:11, where God makes a similar promise to David).

Jeremiah also reports that God goes on to call Israel his "virgin Israel," by whom he will beget children (Jer. 31:4); yet almost in parallel, at v. 20 we hear God saying of Israel, he is "my dear son," my darling child!

So it came about that "virgin Israel," in the person of Mary, representative of all Israel, became the mother of many sons and daughters (Isa. 66:6-9). It happened by the descent and incarnation of the Holy Spirit, which did not "abhor the virgin's womb." Accordingly the Isaianic claim that God was hidden *in* Israel became historical reality (Isa. 45:14c-15 KJV).

One may question why this issue of God as "Mother" should

be raised here at all when Moses does not even mention it. But that fact is itself the answer. The God of Moses is the Rock who does not change. The goddesses of the Moabites, the Ammonites, and others were anathema to Moses, even when their male spouses were known as the "father" of their people (see Deut. 32:6). Thus we today dare not "quarry" in Moses' Song for the notion that the name of God could be that of Mother, or even that of "Father-Mother." If we were to do so, we would be denying the reality of the words of Jesus, "I have made your name known to those whom you gave me" (John 17:6). But we may say with the church father Cyprian and with John Calvin that if God is our Father, then the Church is our Mother. Calvin declares so in both the first and the last edition of his *Institutes* (iv.1.4).

In Deut. 32:18 the emphasis is upon the fact that the first words a baby utters in love are "Mother," "Father" — and that it was these words that Israel had forgotten. It is a pity that Targum Onkelos, ever eager to get rid of anthropomorphisms, renders the term Rock merely by the phrase "the Strong One." We ourselves must never "forget" that very few theologians before the Reformation knew any Hebrew, and so were condemned to believe that the LXX offers us a true representation of the mind of Moses; for all the LXX says is "the God who bore you . . . the God who feeds you."

Accordingly the LXX gives us little guidance about the significance of the pains of childbirth. Moses speaks about the first creation of Israel in terms of just such excruciating pain. Thereupon it is the Hebrew of the book of Isaiah that speaks of the second creation of Israel, its rebirth from the grace, from the womb of God himself as a birth that can come about only through the suffering of God *in* the suffering servant of Isa. 53: "You have made me the Servant who bears your sins" (see George A. F. Knight, *Servant Theology*, at Isa. 43:24).

Some of the church fathers sought to put into human concepts the unspeakable wonder of the majesty and might of God by the *via negativa*, by saying only what God is *not*. God is *not* as human Israel is, foolish, senseless (Deut. 32:6), greedy, self-centered, scoffing at fidelity, grace, love, and care (v. 15). Although the root q-d-sh ("holy") does not occur in the Song, it is inherent in the covenantal formula (Exod. 19:5-6) from which it is taken up by subsequent writers (e.g., "Be holy, for I am holy"; Lev. 11:44). Holiness is the essential perfection of God (Deut. 32:4) that necessarily stands opposed to all idolatry and rebelliousness on mankind's part (v. 12). This is sung about in the even more ancient song at the crossing of the 'Reed' Sea (Exod. 15:11).

Moses then describes the nature of God as holy. He does so by declaring that all God's so-called "attributes" that flow from holiness, such as righteousness, justice, faithfulness, truth, are terms we can use to describe the One who is holy beyond all human imagination. Theologians rightly find in our Song that Moses speaks of two basic qualities of God from which all else derives, namely, holiness and love. Of the latter we shall hear more later at Deut. 32:36. At the moment we are to recognize that God's holiness is not to be viewed as the obverse of Israel's unholiness. Rather God seeks to show forth his holiness *through* Israel; he does so with the missionary purpose that "when they see that I reveal my holiness through you, the nations will know that I am the LORD" (Ezek. 36:23 NEB).

This activity by God we meet with later in the Song. There we learn that God's holiness is not a static quality, but rather is active and creative, even re-creative. So it is that Ps. 51:10-13, following Moses' poem, is able to reveal a human awareness of mankind's moral limitations. It has discovered that holiness in the response to God's holiness in his people Israel must not be static either, but always active, creative, loving. So these verses represent as a corollary the sense of radical joy that comes from the revelation that God, as the Holy One of Israel, is holier and lovelier than anything we human beings can ever imagine (Deut. 32:4).

And all this is what Israel forgot!

vv. 19-20   The LORD saw it, and was jealous,
      he spurned his sons and daughters.
  He said: I will hide my face from them,
      I will see what their end will be;
  for they are a perverse generation,
      children in whom there is no faithfulness.

Yahweh is no mere abstract spirit. Yahweh is the living God, and as such sees, hears, and acts. Such is the terrible warning contained in the explanatory passage in Deut. 31:17 made some centuries later than our Song but first uttered here: "I will hide my face from them."

Described thus in a personal manner Moses declares of God: "He saw." There is no "it" here. The Hebrew sounds much more ominous without it. Again all we have is "he spurned" (better, "rejected"), with no word for "them." What Yahweh did was to separate himself from the whole ugly situation that had resulted from the provocation of his children. The whole nation that was his adopted son is now described as Yahweh's individual sons and daughters because they are the fruit of the "marriage covenant" made at Sinai. It is made clear moreover by this sentence that men and women equally come under the judgment of the living God. It was Israel of course that had instigated the disruption of relations, not God. Here, however, we have the door opening onto the *hemah,* the "wrath," the *orge* of God, since to be forsaken by God is "to stand under his wrath" (cf. Mark 15:34). God is not impersonal Fate, but is the personal God. God's wrath is his Self acting to discipline his sons and his daughters — until they can be restored to his image, as our poem goes on to reveal. And since he is the God of the Covenant, though he has hidden his face from them, it becomes evident that there is no escape from the presence of the living God. At Isa. 54:8 the prophet of the Exile applies God's words at Deut. 32:20 to the situation his people are now in, and develops them in a manner any person in history could appreciate. Today a child, boy or girl, may be adopted into the family of God, but be under no guarantee to remain loyal to the

Covenant. As G. B. Caird remarks, "In the Bible, predestination is never confused with determinism. God's appointments have absolute performative force, but their causal power never dispenses with human response" (*The Language and Imagery of the Bible*, 24). In the same way a person can shut himself off from discovering the ultimate secrets of nature. These will not be revealed till mankind has stopped the self-destructive activity that prevents their seeing what kind of world they are really in. The people that forsakes God, as Jeremiah declares, crumbles into chaos. There is never any suggestion that Israel are "the righteous," or even *some* Israelites. All are sinners and all need redemption.

"He said" — perhaps "said to himself," and so "thought," "planned" — "I will hide. . . ." Such a phrase once again expresses God's subjective experience of pain and horror. But God indeed "says." From the very beginning (Gen. 1:3) God had chosen to reveal himself through saying his Word. He wills, then, to turn his face away from his chosen people, with the result that they no longer see his face, or hear the Word from his mouth, and so can no longer learn of God's nature and character and purpose in naming Israel his sons and his daughters (Gen. 9:15). The later prophets are well aware of this aspect of the nature of God (cf. Isa. 57:17; Jer. 18:17). Targum Onkelos expands this line thus: "I have spoken in my Word to withhold from them my Holy Spirit." We note that the Targum does not seek to distinguish between God's Word and God's Spirit. This is because it is God *in* his Word and God *in* his Spirit of whom mention is made.

Once God "hides his face" from them, Israel's enemies flow into the "spaces" left by the divine withdrawal and Israel is delivered into their hands (Terence E. Fretheim, *The Suffering of God*). What amazes us, however, is that all this happens for Israel's good! Neither Israel nor we (for example in a church service) can repeat, "God is here, blessed be He, according to his promise." This is because we do not "possess" God by inalienable right. God's presence is always a loving gift.

Again because time and eternity are one, as are also matter

and spirit, there is nothing that can possibly separate us from God except sin. It was only after they had sinned that Adam and Eve found that they had hidden themselves from God. Human receptiveness of sin, human experience, can therefore affect the intensity of the divine presence, whereupon God "hides his face from them." As savior from the weight of the enchainment of sin, therefore, Jesus had to experience the hiddenness of God, and on the Cross exclaim, "My God, my God, why have you forsaken me?"

God goes on — or is it Moses? As we saw at Deut. 32:2, we cannot differentiate between the word of Moses and the word of God. How strange it is that the Word of God reaches human ears only through the heart and mind of a fallible human being. In consequence the potentialities of that human person must also experience the pain and frustration embodied in the proclamation of the Word. We must never forget that Moses was united to God by "the blood of the covenant" (Exod. 24:8). Walter Brueggemann brings out this relationship between God and his other prophet Jeremiah with clarity (*To Pluck Up, To Tear Down*).

After he "said," God continues with "I will see . . ." and so experience in my own heart what the "eschatological significance" (*aharit*) of their action will turn out to be (cf. Deut. 31:17); for they are a generation that "reverses" my plans for them. The noun translated "end" comes from the root *ahar*, meaning "behind," "backside," "after." Since the writers of ancient Hebrew seem on occasion to have thought pictorially, we might do well to follow their example and to conceive of the "meaning" of historical events as being visible on the "backside" of the veil that separates this world from the eternal world. God of course can see this meaning, and so is able to enter into the pathos of Moses who can only see events on this side, and so God can enter into Moses' pain. This union between God and mankind is clarified by Deutero-Isaiah, who as we have seen declares at Isa. 45:14-15 that God hides himself *in* Israel (KJV) within all his people's sin and perversity. So God is burdened with Israel's sins. We read literally, "You made me the servant who bears your sins" (Isa. 43:24). Such is theologically possible only because God's wrath is correlative with his holiness and covenantal love. As Pinchas Lapide says, "God's pathos is a free relationship to creation, to God's people and their future. But it is also a relationship of passionate participation" (Lapide and Jürgen Moltmann, *Jewish Monotheism and Christian Trinitarian Doctrine*, 48).

In later books of the Pentateuch God is claimed to have put his "face" *(panim)* in the sanctuary. This anthropomorphic picture term is usually translated in English by the word "presence." Thus the bread of the presence was placed each week before God's "face" as an offering to him. In this way this pictorial theological concept came to acquire a cultic usage — all the more appalling then that this "perverse generation" should dare to "tie God down" in their midst in the sanctuary.

"Perverse" translates a plural noun meaning something like "turned upside down" (see above at Deut. 32:5). They were a generation that had stood God's grace on its head, so to speak. They were children (both sexes) who had no *emun* in them — no trustworthiness, no "faithfulness"; they were not as the Rock that was their covenant partner. Rather they put their trust in demonic powers. The parallel with our day would be to say that, instead of trusting to God's creative and redemptive plan for the world, we put our trust in scientific technology (cf. Isa. 1:3-4; Ps. 78:8; Phil. 2:15), for the root of the word *emun* refers to what is unshakable and secure.

The LXX reads "I will show what will happen to them," for the Hebrew "I will see . . . ," quite changing the sense. For "their end" it has "in the last days," again revealing how a thousand years after Moses the Hellenized Jews of Alexandria sorely misunderstood the emphasis of the Hebrew term *aharit*.

That God hides his face, even when his covenant people are not able to trace the reason why, has been the subject of worried speculation at all times, from the book of Job to the prison experience of Dietrich Bonhoeffer in Adolf Hitler's war. Under the great stress of his imprisonment and probable execution, Bonhoeffer came to realize that in his providence God may choose to let human beings "do without him," clearly in order to force them to examine just what gods they may unwittingly be worshipping — and this even while they really believe they are innocent of any deception of God (cf. Deut. 31:17ff., which the compilers of the whole book of Deuteronomy use as an introduction to "this Song," v. 21). (See Dietrich Bonhoeffer, *Letters and Papers from Prison*, 360. See also Karl Rahner's phrase in *The Practice of Faith:* "the unending desert of God's silence," a phrase which occurs in several forms throughout his works.)

In his *Theology and the Pain of God*, Kazoh Kitamori has interpreted this issue in extenso, especially in his chapter entitled "The Pain of God and the Hidden God" (105-116). Kitamori writes, "The concept of the 'hidden God' can be realized only in the sense of 'love rooted in the pain of God'" (112). This love of his rooted in his pain is his grace and mercy (112). It is quite awesome to discover that from the very beginning of the Covenant relationship between God and Israel God has revealed himself in the same terms as he does in the Cross of Christ. Karl Rahner adds, "This is because in his pathos God himself becomes a covenant partner of Israel's punishment pain."

We must take both sides of the expression "the word of God" or "God said" seriously, according to Raymond E. Brown (*The Critical Meaning of the Bible*, 1). "It is a human word, for God does not speak. But it is *of* God, and not simply a human composition about God." Moreover, since it is the living God who "says," what he says must be alive as God is alive. What God says to Moses does not end there. His words "I will hide my face" must continue to confront each new generation of Israelites, the people of the Covenant. And since God has never abandoned his Covenant nor rejected his people (Rom. 11:1), the power of the Word is present in the life of the people of God today as truly as ever. This reality the Pharisees of the Gospels did not understand. They said, "We have Moses, that is enough." But Moses would have remained fossilized in the time warp of the ancient world, if it were not that God had addressed Moses with his *living* Word.

Then again since the Word is one of pain, "the experience of the divine *pathos* opens human beings for full love: they love with the love of God; they are angry with the anger of God; they suffer with the suffering of God; they rejoice with the joy of God." Pinchas Lapide comes back to this "cardinal question": "Why did God create the world?" The Talmud's answer is that "God created it out of love." Why? "Because love is the only thing which has need of a partner, and therefore God created humankind in God's image" (Lapide and Moltmann, *Jewish Monotheism and Christian Trinitarian Doctrine*, 65, 348).

So our anchor as we seek to understand Deut. 32:20 is that the Moses who sang it had been made aware at the very beginning (Exod. 3:12) that even God did not seem to be *there* at all. Rather he was there *for* his servant Moses in the latter's deepest awareness.

Ultimately then in our case, when we are tempted to suppose that God has turned his back upon us, we do so because, in the words of Paul van Buren, we lack the audacity to see God precisely in the suffering and the failure of the Cross. "God steps back to leave us free to work his will, if we will, and suffers with us in all our failures. Therein lies the power and the majesty of his infinite freedom — free to sit still and to suffer in agony as his children move so slowly to exercise what he has willed for them" (*A Christian Theology of the People Israel*).

> v. 21   They made me jealous with what is no god,
>   provoked me with their idols.
>   So I will make them jealous with what is no people,
>   provoke them with a foolish nation.

Verse 20 has described God's negative response to Israel's perversity. Now, however, v. 21 goes on to describe the posi-

tive response God makes, in action, deriving out of the negation.

The first line reveals something of the profundity of God's
nature and purpose that Moses is seeking to probe. How could
God be literally "aroused to heat" unless by being confronted
by at least another god? But here God lets himself be stirred to
"jealousy," "zeal," "passion," by "what is no god" (cf. Ps. 5:5-6).

Here the concept of marital infidelity is hinted at. Israel has
not only "grieved" God; they have made him furiously angry.
The terms used here are employed frequently in later prophetic
writings when these accuse Israel of "going awhoring after other
gods." This is patently "covenantal" language in that the Sinai
covenant is interpreted in terms of a marriage between God
and Israel (cf. Isa. 45:25; 54:5; Jer. 3:1, 13).

Jealousy is not the mean, narrow emotion we suppose it to
be. The root of the term means "darkened," so it applies to the
complexion of the face when one displays a strong emotion.
The Hebrew adjective can thus best be translated by "zealous"
rather than "jealous." In a word God "feels" Israel's apostasy
intensely. We have seen that as the father of a rebellious child
God's heart is broken. To use the other figure of the God-Israel
relationship that Hosea (ch. 11) puts together with the marriage
of his early chapters, God discovers that he has been cuckolded.
No wonder God in his wrath declares, "*They* have provoked
me."

It is only his holy zeal that allows God to respond in this
way, to the extent of letting his covenant people discover existentially what it feels like for God to suffer their provocation
of him. "No people" becomes a wordplay on "no god" (cf. Hos.
1:9). Actually "made me jealous" is a pun in Hebrew (*qn', qnh*)
upon the verb "bear, beget" (*yld*, Deut. 32:18). So the Hebrew
ear picked up God's ludicrous cry: "I will 'beget' them as no
people!" Could such a thing be possible?

In a sense this is a theological interpretation of the striking
pronouncement in the Mosaic legislation, "an eye for an eye"
(Exod. 21:24), which is scorned by modern, Western, secular

people as being merely "primitive vengeance." But Yahweh is the God of pure justice. No picture of total judgment surpasses that in 2 Kgs. 21:13: "I will wipe Jerusalem as one wipes a dish, wiping it and turning it upside down." However, what Moses is heralding in this sermon-song is that God is the God of pure justice and at the same time of absolute mercy, and as we read on we must keep these two emphases firmly in view.

In Deut. 32:21 Moses moves forward from his description of God's special relationship to Israel by declaring that he is LORD of all peoples. Yahweh's activities are not confined to Israel alone (see Amos 1–3). Moses does not handle our modern concept of *Heilsgeschichte* ("saving history") as if it were a historical movement apart from the nations of mankind. Amos again makes the same emphasis on the basis of the Song of Moses (Amos 9:7; Obad. 2). Nor does Moses suggest that God is under any absolute necessity to proceed in the way he does. God's action is freely chosen, based as it is in his own essential freedom of will; otherwise mankind would never have known what their particular freedom of will was — freedom to obey or freedom to live their own self-chosen, egotistical manner of life.

"They . . . provoked me with their idols" *(hebel)*. This is the noun used repeatedly in the book of Ecclesiastes, traditionally translated "vanity." Israel's gods were vacuous, inane, empty, evanescent concepts (cf. Isa. 57:13). Instead of putting God first in their lives and remaining faithful to him they had filled their God-given lives with empty wind; and because these winds were "no gods" Israel had become "no-Israel," that is, inhuman, the reverse of having been created in the image of God. God's holy zeal, on the other hand, showed itself steadfastly as his unspeakable longing and desire to keep Israel faithful to the covenant with himself. For of course Israel receives its life from the living God alone. That meant God revealed his zeal to keep his people from adultery, that is, from going awhoring after other gods. God's purpose was to teach them in practical human life-situations what it meant for them in their turn to be stirred to anger at the attitude of some other neighboring nations who had perhaps proved to be disloyal to Israel (cf. Amos 1:9).

God continues: As for me I will do this: "*I* will provoke them with a *goi nabal.*" *Goi* is a gentile nation. Israel on the other hand is invariably described as God's *'am.* As we saw at Deut. 32:6 *nabal* means much more than just "foolish." It is foolishness bordering on viciousness (cf. Ps. 74:18).

This is the way it has been historically all down the ages. Time and time again God has felt it necessary to "provoke" some godless "vandal" nation — Babylonians, Goths, Huns, Norsemen, whatever (in fact, Targum Onkelos interpreted "a foolish nation" as the Babylonians) — to attack his own covenant people, recognizing that only by so doing can he reveal to them the enormity of their behavior in "vandalizing" the Covenant of Grace. Paul makes use of this piece of Mosaic theology at Rom. 10:19-21.

> v. 22　For a fire is kindled by my anger,
> 　　　　　and burns to the depths of Sheol;
> 　　　it devours the earth and its increase,
> 　　　　　and sets on fire the foundations of the mountains.

We now listen to God's declaration of war. Moses introduces the picture of fire in order to reveal the nature of God's wrath. Fire in itself is a reality that is either destructive or else purifies what it seems to destroy. Here it would seem to be both at once, which is an idea we human creatures are not able to hold together as one. The book of Deuteronomy takes up the figure of God as fire more than once. At Deut. 4:24 we read: "For the LORD your God is a devouring fire, a jealous God"; Isa. 10:17; 33:14; Mal. 4:1 raise the issue again. But the concept is always personalized in the Hebrew. For example, the fire comes forth from God's nostrils even as he snorts in wrath (Ps. 18:8 = 2 Sam. 22:9). Here our line uses a vivid assonance, with phonetically similar words set in parallel with each other in the Hebrew: "For a fire is *kindled* in my nostrils; it *burns* to the depths of Sheol." Dante's Inferno was conjured up within the climate of thought that positioned hell deep under the earth, since the ancient Hebrews had placed Sheol there (Gen. 37:35; Amos 9:2; Ps. 86:13). Moreover, in our era with its strong commitment to scientific exactitude, we are being warned by Moses that the expression "sets on fire the foundations of the mountains" is not a scientific statement but is rather an instance of "theology in pictures."

In early Israel simple people evidently believed Sheol to be a real place. This was because they were under the enormous pressure of Canaanite and Egyptian concepts that virtually held them in chains. Moses did not dismiss their superstitions as unworthy of taking seriously. Rather he used their ideology to convey to them a theological truth. We see the same today where any good church people are unwilling to recognize that they are held in the chains of neo-Platonic scientific secularism.

Sheol, of course, is not a "place" at all. It is the theological concept of the "not land," of the chaos of "nonbeing" that is pictured in Gen. 1:2. It is only *shalom*, which is not a place either — the wholeness and fullness of God's plan for his creation — that is "really real." Sheol is the "not land" to be understood in parallel with the "no people" of Deut. 32:21.

Remembering all this, we are given the correct answer to the false, humanistic approach to the person of Christ which has led commentators at times to be unsure of how to interpret John the Baptist's declaration that Jesus had come to "baptize you with the Holy Spirit and fire . . . the chaff he will burn with unquenchable fire" (Matt. 3:11-12) and the words of Jesus himself: "I came to bring fire to the earth" (Luke 12:49).

"The consuming fire image in both Testaments points to the inexhaustibility of the divine, the fire that is never exhausted — the bush that burns but never burns up" (James A. Carpenter, *Nature and Grace*, 71; cf. Exod. 3:2). Carpenter adds, "God's inner being is inexhaustible and cannot be exhaustively revealed." Yet, paradoxically, it is revealed fully and completely in the person of Jesus. Jesus' frequently uttered words "Woe unto you . . ." reveal that his mind is fully in accord with that of God.

Since there were in all probability no atheists in the ancient world, such questions as "Is the LORD among us or not?" and "Has not the LORD wrought all this" are the nearest we can get to Israel's asking "Does Yahweh really exist?" If the Song is posing the doubting question whether God is indeed ultimate truth, then it has the courage to include within it the debate over God's existence. The answer comes that God is the power that determines everything. This is revealed to us in the poem's demonstration of God's lordship over all creation (cf. Job 42:1-3). Yahweh is LORD not only over us sinful mortals, but over all creation as one whole. In this way a relationship is drawn between mankind and nature. God is Creator. Through his wisdom God *planted* Israel (Deut. 32:32) as a vine. By this logic, then, Moses interprets past and present to form what is actually a doctrine.

Israel, then, does not reject belief in the existence of God. Israel rejects belief that God's "total plan" of redemption could affect the totality of creation. Sin is not a private indiscretion. God's fire burns down to the depths of Sheol, to the abode of the dead. In other words it even affects the ancestors of Israel, Abraham, Isaac, Jacob, and Sarah. And God "kindles" it — deliberately! This is a terrible thought. God's fire devours the created earth and all that lives upon it, its "increase" (*yebul*). This word means something like "interest." The earth is God's capital gift to mankind. What it produces and what human beings are meant to produce from it is the interest on the capital.

God's anger "sets on fire the foundations of the mountains," even though these "float" upon the primal depths of chaos (Ps. 46:2-3). The statement invites us to recognize that God's judgment goes back to the creation of time as well as of space, time and space being wholly integrated as Gen. 1:4 shows us. God created time only when he separated light from darkness. Such a concept mankind finds is beyond them to correlate with a claim such as is expressed by Deutero-Isaiah at Isa. 51:16: "[While I was] stretching out the heavens and laying the foundations of the earth, [I was] saying to Zion, 'You are my people.'" This is followed by Paul at Eph. 1:4. But then, all God does is of grace!

Now since God had created both space and time, it meant that God could and probably would bring his creation to an end. But God himself is the rock of ages, and not part of that creation. God is beyond both time and space, so that beyond the end he will still be God. In the here and now, however, the realm of the Spirit is equally present at all times and places, like the rainbow arch of God's compassion and covenant care that Noah saw around him once God had rescued him from the waters of chaos (Gen. 9:12-13). This means that the "other world" is always present both above and beneath the flow of history. As just one verse of another very ancient poem puts it (Deut. 33:27 MT): "The God who goes ahead (*qedem*, or 'who has been from the beginning') is [your] dwelling place" (even though you may also dwell in the Holy Land), and "underneath are the everlasting (*'olam*) arms," the arms of the eternal God.

So Deut. 32:22 leads us to discover an unspeakably moving and paradoxical reality about the nature of God. "A fire is kindled *in* my anger" (in my nose — a very personal idea, just as are the words "everlasting arms"), and it "burns to the depths of Sheol; it devours the earth" (the "capital" that God has "lent" us) and what it has produced (the "interest" mankind has made from it; cf. Matt. 18:23-25), "and sets on fire the foundations of the mountains," exactly where the everlasting arms hold all in their loving embrace. But we ended a previous paragraph by saying that "all God does is of grace!"

This view of the totality of God's rule was lost in later centuries to the consciousness of Israel in the so-called Persian period after the return from exile. The Persians held the notion that there were two worlds, and that heaven and hell were completely other than this world of human history. But what we meet with here is a concept unique to the OT, that God's wrath is an unremitting expression of his reaction to the attack of sin upon his holiness (Deut. 32:18). It is interesting to note that Moses' affirmation of the timelessness of God (v. 40) was enunciated seven hundred years before Plato thought to suggest the timelessness of creation.

This then is what the Almighty *could* do, and what in justice God *ought* to do as a consequence of Israel's sin. In a vision of horror the young Jeremiah actually "saw" just this total reversal of creation taking place (Jer. 4:23-26), again as a just consequence of Israel's apostasy and for spurning their election to be God's coworker for the rehabilitation of creation. Amazingly this included responsibility for being God's choice of Israel as his instrument for the rehabilitation of creation. Amos put it succinctly: "You only have I known (in the sense of sexual union in marriage) of all the families of the earth; therefore I will punish you . . ." (Amos 3:2).

We should recognize then that this whole section, Deut. 32:22-25, is not a literal threat of what God is about to do to his people. It represents pictorially what would be a just punishment for Israel's apostasy, in that the latter had cosmic significance. It is a warning of the precariousness of Israel's very existence, so that Israel's only hope can be for a total reliance upon God's grace. At the same time the passage is a warning of how God actually handles and makes use of human suffering. Suffering can destroy, but it can also bring out the best qualities in human nature. Thus God must necessarily be cruel in order to be kind if he is to go forward with his plan of recreating humanity in his own likeness. In their suffering, then, mankind comes to live by hope that the future holds the outcome of all that they must undergo (cf. Eccl. 3:11). But first mankind must drink the cup of wrath (Jer. 25:15ff.) before they can be handed the cup of salvation (Ps. 16:5; 116:13). Several centuries later the main section of the book of Deuteronomy takes up Moses' thesis and lays great stress upon the blessing or the cursing God must lay before his chosen people (cf. Deut. 30:15-20).

Historically speaking, however, God employs "fire" to fall not only upon his own people but upon the pagan nations as well (Amos 1). Amos warns that "the end" has come upon "my people Israel" (Amos 8:2), as it did in fact in the year 587 when Jerusalem fell to the might of the Babylonian armies, or as happened at the destruction of Jerusalem by the Romans in A.D. 70. Jesus taught that inevitable event was a "type" of God's judgment on the world order as a whole. In this sense Deut. 32 is "prophecy," for prophecy is the discernment of the underlying purpose of contemporary events which it carries with it into the pattern and goal of history.

Again what we have here is that God does not pursue his plan "in a straight line." One never knows in which direction the Word will move, declares Gerhard von Rad. The kingdom of God does not "evolve" smoothly, gradually, and inevitably just because God is almighty and so could feasibly act in such a manner. The kingdom dawns through crises. In the book of Judges Israel's final settlement in Canaan comes about only through a series of forty-year cycles of disobedience, pain, and disillusionment. Each time God must rescue his people from the powers of evil, only to have to begin all over again. If Moses sings his Song primarily for Joshua's sake, he is seeking to give him theological insight into the realities he will have to face once across the Jordan. There life is not left totally ungoverned. God "preserves" his creation, human and beast together (Ps. 36:6; cf. 104:29-30). The fire of God's wrath must therefore be an aspect of his governance, his providence, his "economy." It must belong in that area of God's "hidden face" (Deut. 32:20) which is turned away from our sight and understanding, yet which must lead to God's final act of redemption both of Israel and of all creation (v. 43). In a sense then both good and evil proceed from God (Isa. 45:7), both of which are elements of God's free, abundant, and gracious love which is his ultimate answer to our human state of sin. God *permits* us to "grow fat and kick," but God does not *permit* evil to rule over us ultimately; for in his own good time God overrules our rebellion by an act of grace (cf. Deut. 32:36; Gen. 50:20).

vv. 23-24   I will heap disasters upon them,
　　　　　　　　spend my arrows against them;
　　　　　　wasting hunger,
　　　　　　　　burning consumption,
　　　　　　　　bitter pestilence.
　　　　　The teeth of beasts I will send against them,
　　　　　　　with venom of things crawling in the dust.

The picture is now of what God's judgment ought to do to Israel apart from any judgment upon the rest of creation. Targum Onkelos now picks up the words "he said" of v. 20 and so continues: "I have spoken in my Word to array calamities against them." As Moses declares in v. 21, such a retribution God has "foreordained" for them. Yet even such preordination is subject to the unalterable compassion of God to save and to recreate (v. 36). Thus God may even *prevent* the outworking of his "inevitable" judgment from harming the sinner such as happened in the case of Abraham (Gen. 20:6).

"I will heap (or 'sweep up,' or possibly 'add') disasters upon them." Whichever is the correct rendering of the Hebrew consonants, we are to note that it is God who initiates the judgment. What God does is to take the existing evils Israel has wrought (the "bank interest," the *yebul* they have gained) and add them on to the heap, the mess they have produced (cf. Ps. 7:14-16). Such punishment is later incorporated into the Law of Holiness at Lev. 26:21-26, possibly through Ezek. 5:16-17. This phrase "I will . . ." suggests a continuous creative action, so as to allow evil to exist that good may emerge from it.

Hebrew *ra'ot* covers all kinds of evil, catastrophes, diseases, sin (there is no line between them), human enemies, natural disasters — the whole world of chaos against which God is always at war. There is a seventeenth-century saying: "War, pest, and famines are the three scourges of God." In the later literature of the OT God's arrows are usually pictured as shafts of lightning, these being his own choice of weapons. The Greek Version develops the picture: "I will cause my weapons to war together against them." This development may have arisen from the sense of the Hebrew verb "spend," which can make this sense of the phrase: "I will use them all up (the arrows in my quiver) in a pitiless shower."

Yet is there not here a hint of God's *hesed*, his "steadfast love" (cf. Ps. 136)? Even when God has spent all his arrows, and when there are none left, Israel will still be there. But before that there comes a point in God's providence and creative love where God must let Israel go, as at Judg. 10:13: "You have abandoned me and worshiped other gods; therefore I will deliver you no more" (cf. Jer. 12:8; Rom. 1:28). And yet God still holds on to Israel in covenant!

Walter Brueggemann writes of the time of Jeremiah: "The judgment of God is no doubt stereotypical and hyperbolic. Its massive, relentless force is necessary to penetrate the complacent self-assurance of Judah that 'it can't happen here.' This prophetic speech makes the harsh claim: 'it can and it will'" (*To Pluck Up, To Tear Down*, 169).

Deut. 32:24 now lists the evils threatened in v. 23. The pitiless shower brings starvation upon human beings. There follows suffering from the enervating heat of a waterless desert, from being bitten by poisonous serpents, from being devoured by wild beasts, from the venom ("wrath") of crawling things. "Wasting" means being virtually "sucked dry," "emptied out," a usage occurring again only at Isa. 5:13. The Hebrew translated "burning consumption" (*resheph*; RSV "devoured with burning heat") means to be "consumed with fever." This phrase could also be rendered "conquered by Reseph," the Ugaritic god of pestilence mentioned in the Ras Shamra texts contemporary with Moses. In the same way one could speak of the Black Death in medieval Europe or the AIDS threat today.

We continue: "bitter pestilence" is expressed by two Hebrew words, "cut off" and "poisonous" meaning probably "total pestilence," thus describing what we would regard as an epidemic. Of course Yahweh is LORD of both sickness and healing

(v. 39). "Crawling things" remind us of maggots and worms (cf. Mic. 7:17). The idea of "teeth" is enough to give us a shiver of horror, as when today we only need cry "Shark!" to create such a response. Deutero-Isaiah incorporates God's words here into his argument at Isa. 42:24-25. Ezekiel for one has mined and quarried this Song for illustrations he can use in the terrible days of the destruction of Jerusalem through which he lived (Ezek. 5:16; 14:21; cf. also Lam. 3:1-18).

We recall that according to Gen. 1 the beasts of the field are brought forth by natural reproduction. "Adam" — man and woman together — alone is created by the Word of the LORD. God "said" — and humankind was. Humankind has no context; it is not related to the mammals; rather, as "male and female" humankind is created "in the image of God." Yet as this verse indicates, God employs the natural animal world to discipline them whom he has created in his own image. To decide to do this with his marvelous creation which God saw to be "very good" (Gen. 1:31) must have been an agonizing experience for the living God. No wonder, as Isa. 63:15 puts it, God experiences "the sounding of thy bowels" (KJV), pain throughout his whole inner being.

All this did actually happen to Israel at various times throughout its history; and so in a sense the history of Israel became the history of God. Consequently God's history continued on through the Incarnation, the Cross, and the Resurrection in Christ (2 Cor. 5:19) in continuity with this vision of Moses.

In For All Mankind, Stuart Blanch writes, "There is only one theology, and that is the theology of the Old Testament. Jesus, Paul and the other Apostles knew no other theology. . . . The New Testament does not alter that theology one whit, it simply points it up and announces that God's purpose, once seen to be effective in the life of Israel, was now to be seen as supremely effective in a particular member of that race, Jesus of Nazareth" (89). It is only because this generation of scholarship, typified by Blanch, has been made aware of the unity of the two Testaments, that the reality of God's pain (as at the Cross) has been the subject of deep study by such theologians as Jürgen Moltmann, *The Crucified God;* Terence E. Fretheim, *The Suffering of God;* and Kazoh Kitamori, *Theology and the Pain of God.*

In Job 33 Elihu, one of Job's friends, develops the main thrust of the verses we are examining, pointing his argument straight at Job, for Job cannot discern any sense in the "cruel" ways of God. Elihu points out that God must in fact be "cruel to be kind," otherwise Job would not know what redemption meant, and so finally God's own love cures Job of his mental depression, his "descent into Sheol."

The point is that there is a "constant" to be seen throughout the OT from Moses onwards. It is the revelation that there is a demonic antidivine principle at work in and with all God's dealings with his people. Yet this demonic element participates in the divine power of grace (J. S. Whale, *Victor and Victim*). Isaiah knew of it when he spoke of God's "alien" work (Isa. 28:21), even though it is linked with God's "proper" work of salvation (v. 16). Finally, however, the two are seen as one in the cross of Christ.

The binding link that leads directly from Moses to Paul, through the whole maze of God's proper and alien work, is what Moses called *the* covenant and Paul calls the *ancient (palaios)* covenant. This Greek word does not mean old, out-of-date, and ready to be displaced. This we recognize when we note that Paul's word for "new" is not *neos,* something qualitatively different, but *kainos.* By this last word Paul translates Heb. *hadash,* the word used to describe the new moon, which coming up fresh each month is always the same old, ancient moon! In other words, just as there is only one theology that binds the OT to the NT, so there is only one Covenant, that which both Moses and Paul sought to serve. The New *(kaine)* Covenant (or "Testament" as in Latin) is thus the ancient, original *(palaios)* Covenant given at Sinai, refurbished, recreated, re-empowered in the life, death, and resurrection of Jesus Christ (cf. also Rom. 11:28-33).

v. 25   In the street the sword shall bereave,
      and in the chambers terror,
    for young man and woman alike,
      nursing child and old gray head.

God's wrath is now pinpointed on the ordinary people of Israel. We have a picture of cavalrymen on horseback cutting down civilians with their swords on a city's streets, and of families crouching in terror within their homes. All classes of citizens fall before the sword, teenage lads, young women with babies in their arms, and gray-haired old women and men. Having sat at Moses' feet Joshua would believe that his wars, cruel as they were, were under the overall economy of God (Josh. 5:13-15; cf. also Ps. 78:53-55; Amos 2:9; Acts 13:16-19). Joshua could and did make horrible mistakes in his tactics, yet even these mistakes God *used* by weaving their outcome into his overall developing plan.

"The sword shall bereave" — but whose sword? The sword held in human hands. What Moses is saying is that unless you love God first you do not know what it means to love your neighbor. Internecine strife, international wars, and the destruction of the inhabitants of Jericho occur only when human beings suppose that their own lusts, greed, and ambitions are what are naturally meant to rule their lives. But a person such as Joshua must be aware that, through the covenant given at Sinai, God has revealed that he is "in love" with Israel. The human response of love to God then precedes a person's approach to his or her neighbor, for one cannot love his neighbor unless one loves God first.

Moses recognizes that a person cannot stand against evil any more than against a steamroller. One cannot overcome evil without society suffering, including babes in arms, for we are all bound up together in the bundle of life (1 Sam. 25:29). That is our abstraction of the issue, however. The OT prefers a battlefield picture to represent God's war against evil. God's war took place in Moses' day, but it is also being conducted *now*, in fact at every "now." Morton Smith declares that between Alexander the Great's death in 323 and the conquest of Palestine by Pompey in 63 B.C. "there were at least 200 campaigns fought in or across Palestine" (*Palestinian Parties*, 63ff.). So, while war is not the will of the God of love, God *uses* mankind's wars to get his will done in the world.

So then God *uses* war. God is *in* Joshua's wars. God is even ready "to get his hands dirty." God is willing to "look bad" to us as he uses mankind's evil ways and accommodates them into his plan (cf. 1 Cor. 1:26-31). "God has given up absolute power to this end so as not to violate the integrity of the established relationship" (Terence E. Fretheim, *The Suffering of God*, 76).

Perhaps we may conclude this section of the Song by reflecting that wrath is the prerogative of God alone. This is because God's is the wrath of pure holiness. Mankind is not holy, therefore men and women may not, dare not, think to possess and exercise wrath on their own. God alone is Judge. Mankind cannot judge in the divine sense; they are precluded from doing so in that they are self-centered and self-righteous. As Jesus put it: "Do not judge, so that you may not be judged" (Matt. 7:1). God alone may conduct a "holy war" against the powers of evil.

The poem points here to the ethical problem (from our point of view) as to why young boys and girls, even babes in arms, have to suffer for the sins of their grandparents. But as the poem continues and we reach the climax at its end, we are content to recognize that while wicked people perform the massacre, it is done "according to the definite plan and foreknowledge of God" (cf. Acts 2:23). For it is a basic constituent in God's plan that God should overrule for good even the most terrible atrocities that humans, because of their free will, can choose to perform upon their fellow humans. This then is what Isa. 28:21 calls "God's strange work"; or, as Martin Luther expressed it in the theological terms of his day, it is God's *opus alienum*.

vv. 26-27   I thought to scatter them
        and blot out the memory of them
          from humankind;
      but I feared provocation by the enemy,
        for their adversaries might misunderstand
    and say, "Our hand is triumphant;
        it was not the LORD who did all this."

We have now reached the turning point of the Song. That in it Moses sings of revelation, and not of "law" or of "morals," is emphasized for the young Jeremiah who would know this Song possibly even by heart, so basic is it as a word from God. In his preaching (Jer. 1) Jeremiah was "to pluck up and to pull down, to destroy and to overthrow," and only then "to build and to plant" (see Walter Brueggemann, *To Pluck Up, To Tear Down*, 24). Brueggemann writes, "The issue turns on whether Yahweh really governs, because that governance is always slow, always invisible, always capable of other explanation" (29).

The translation of ancient Hebrew verbal tenses is notoriously difficult. Classical Hebrew did not possess such shades of meaning as we can express by "would," "could," "should," and so on. Deut. 32:20 has newly stated, "He said," the "he" being God. Here in v. 26 then God himself is speaking in the first person in the Hebrew perfect tense. All that the Hebrew has here is "I said." The RSV translates "I would have said"; NEB "I had resolved"; the TEV simply omits. If we take the Hebrew at its face value it could mean "I said within myself," "I thought" (so NRSV), "I planned" (cf. Gen. 6:5-7; Hos. 6:4; 11:8). Then we are given the unique experience of hearing "a detailed deliberation in the heart of God" (Gerhard von Rad, *Deuteronomy*, 198), "a soliloquy within the depths of the divine heart." Unfortunately Targum Onkelos interprets weakly thus: "I have spoken in my Word to withhold from them my Holy Spirit."

The next two verbs are also not precise. They could be rendered "I will scatter" (RSV), "I could" or "might scatter"; "I could (or 'might') make the remembrance of them cease among humankind" by crushing them to dust, rendering them no longer visible as human persons (Exod. 32:10).

Depending from what root the verb "scatter" derives, some suggest it means "split" or "screw," others "dash in pieces"; others again suggest "cleave in pieces." Whichever is correct, the verb must mean something terrible and final. Then again "humankind" here is not the usual *adam*, but *enosh*. This word for "mankind" is found at Gen. 4:26, where it implies that the "humanity" described by this term lived a life of awareness of God, that in fact they were "religious" people.

The verb "scatter," whatever it means, must mark that total justice in the heart of the living God which he must inevitably exhibit and exercise. We hear about *God's* action here, not mankind's, witnessed to by Peter at Acts 2:23. But what we actually have is an agonized soliloquy in the depths of the divine heart, for Yahweh's honor is now at stake. The best rendering therefore is the NRSV's "I thought to. . . ." For if (1) God "says" (RSV) and so passes judgment by means of his Word, how is it that in the same breath (2) God puts Israel's sins behind his back? For (3) by so doing God reveals that to do such with human sins is to put human beings behind his back. Sins are neither "things" nor "objects"; they are not even nouns. The reality of sins normally expressed by verbs is that they are not separable from their perpetrators, for sins are always *people sinning*.

Moreover, the complete destruction of Israel by God would be misinterpreted by Israel's enemies. The latter would not recognize that "all the time it was I who was stirring up the enemy's indignation; I don't want these enemies of Israel to discover that it was I who was doing it and not they themselves, as if it were their own good idea."

We are to recall at this point that Moses' theology on this issue was probably formed in his mind by his encounter with the army of the Amalekites (Exod. 17:8-16). It was the Amalekites who took the initiative and who attacked Israel unprovoked. They did so just when the ordinary people had been ready to stone Moses, and in so doing had actually rebelled against God's leading. The Israelites had "tested the LORD, saying, 'Is the LORD among us or not?'" (Exod. 17:7), whereupon Amalek attacked Israel and fought with them at Rephidim, the "place of giants." In Israel's memory this was the place gigantic issues were at stake, events of eschatological significance; this was because with hindsight they recognized that Amalek was the type of God's enemy throughout the succeeding centuries. Yet even though Israel just before the battle had failed Yahweh, Yahweh did not fail Israel; God rescued them by enabling them to win the battle (cf. Deut. 9:22-29).

As a fact of history, then, Yahweh had not as yet "scattered them," although as he says here he could have annihilated them there and then by heaping upon them those evils listed in Deut. 32:23-25. We should not follow the RSV by translating the first word of v. 26 by "I *would* have said." God *must* destroy his rebellious people, because he is the God of justice, total and absolute — what is summed up in his Torah in the phrase "an eye for an eye." But if God had done so the nations would never have heard the name of Israel, and God's plan for the redemption of the world through his covenant with Israel would have come to a full stop, by *God's* own disloyalty — not Israel's!

The nature and significance of the Amalekites in God's plan is understandable in terms of Satan's relationship to God in the prologue to the book of Job. There we read that God considered using Satan to destroy Job's life, but refused to order it (Job 1:12).

If Israel's enemies had been employed to destroy Israel, then those very enemies would never have had the chance to discover that there is a divine ordering of history, that there is a creative purpose in God's having made a covenant with Israel, and most particularly that "in a weak moment" God does not simply wave a wand over mankind's evil nature and forget it.

First, then, Yahweh manifests himself as LORD of history, as LORD of all the nations of the earth. If any of these had wiped

Israel out, then they would have believed that they or their gods had done it: "Our hand is triumphant" — it was not Yahweh who did "all this" (pa'al). We stress this word pa'al ("work") because when used of God it becomes the poetic term to describe the manifestation of God's power. Thus we could say, even at this point in the argument, God has planned to vindicate and save his rebellious people; yes, and the Gentiles too. God has planned to turn any brutal and negative gentile intervention into a blessing for the peoples of the whole earth.

Second, in so determining Yahweh has taken up the sufferer in order to bring him comfort and to bring shame to his enemies. (Whether the sufferer is responsible for the evil he has wrought or not is now not the question.) Thus when we learn later that "God so loved . . ." we are led to see just how much God does love.

Third, this verse gives us a glimpse of the pain that is ever present in the heart of God. As Ezekiel again and again developed this theme, he concluded that God can only act for his own name's sake (e.g., Ezek. 20:44). God must abide by his own integrity. God can only act with compassion when he ought to act in judgment. In a word, God's choice of action toward silly, superficial, stupid Israel (Deut. 32:28) is evidence that, as Paul put it, "God's foolishness is wiser than human wisdom" (1 Cor. 1:25). As we find here, God is "foolish" to be faithful to his own integrity.

Fourth, God can actually employ human greed to serve his plan. At Judg. 3:12 we read that "the LORD strengthened King Eglon of Moab against Israel, because they had done what was evil in the sight of the LORD." Thus despite the boast of the enemy, the LORD had indeed wrought all this!

Fifth, because Yahweh can only be true to his name, in himself God cannot change; God must be the same yesterday, today, and forever — but, with pain in his heart, God may change his plan! The verb niham ("be sorry, repent," as at Gen. 6:6) is not used here, though later writers develop the term on the basis of Moses' Song. What does not change is God's freedom to act as he chooses to act. What we find here then is that God may will to change his procedure within the contingencies of history because of his never-changing grace. And so, on the basis of Israel's *faithlessness*, God will bring about *restoration* through his own *pathos* (Brueggemann, *To Pluck Up, To Tear Down*, 45).

vv. 28-29   They are a nation void of sense;
        there is no understanding in them.
    If they were wise, they would understand this;
        they would discern what the end would be.

The RSV employs quotation marks here, but the NRSV does not. Who then is speaking, God or Moses — a problem we have met with before. Again, "they . . ." Who are "they?" Evidently Israel is meant, even though the word used for "nation" is Heb. *goi*, meaning any non-Israelite people. Israel had evidently opted out of the covenant relationship. But while Israel may reject Yahweh, Yahweh does not reject Israel. In what follows we find God mitigating Israel's treachery, seeking to explain it and understand it in love and forgiveness. It is interesting that the Damascus Document (5:11b-19), one of the Dead Sea Scrolls, quotes this verse, perhaps through Isa. 27:11c. As Deut. 32:33 is quoted also, it would seem that our Song was lying before the author of the Damascus Document.

    The verb form in the expression "void of sense" (RSV "counsel"), *obed*, means "perishing from having wandered away" from it. The OT offers us many words for sin, but this idea is basic to the most common of those verbs, *hata*, usually translated in the NT by Gk. *hamartanein*. It means aiming at the wrong goal in life, missing the mark. The rabbis said they were void of counsel because they had lost the Torah, meaning the Book of the Covenant, that section of the Torah for which Moses was directly responsible. According to later legislation "sins of inadvertence" could be expiated for by the appropriate sin offerings. Such sins are the kind that Paul refers to when he says, "I do not understand my own actions. For I do not do what I want, but I do the very thing I hate" (Rom. 7:15).

What we have here is a revelation of God's grace. The indictment of stupidity has a sadness to it. Yet we have already been told how heinous Israel's sin is and how it is much more than mere stupidity. God graciously treats it as a sin of inadvertence for which, according to the Torah, there is expiation by the mercy of God. Leviticus goes on to separate sins of inadvertence (Lev. 4:1–5:13) from "sins with a high hand." This phrase offers us a picture of a person holding his dagger on high over his victim with deliberate intent to murder him. Leviticus places rape in the same category as murder, for while murder kills the body, rape destroys the psyche.

We turn to the NT. When Jesus was actually being murdered on the Cross, he was praying to the Father: "Father, forgive them; *for they are only committing a sin of inadvertence*" (Luke 23:34).

Here also then divine grace is revealed to our eyes. How different is Yahweh's reaction to disobedience from that of all-powerful Baal or Chemosh. These delighted in using their power to wreak vengeance upon their frail worshippers when they were "void of sense." Yahweh's power is revealed in his powerlessness to influence Israel by "holding himself in," and that surely is God's glory (see also Isa. 29:13-17).

"Void of sense" meant that they had not turned their minds to thinking through and applying God's counsel (*'etsah*), his plan, in that they had been called to be a kingdom of priests to the world of nations, the *goyim*. This is impressed upon the reader by repetition in various ways. If only they were wise they would *yaskilu* this, show lives of effective knowledge (NRSV "understand"). With regard to the servant the verb is translated at Isa. 52:13 as "prosper." This was because Israel would discover what God's eternal plan was for them "behind the veil." God expects his people to be theologically minded and to use the brains he has given them to think about the meaning and purpose of their election, a point noted at Deut. 32:27.

This expectation is what the Wisdom writers demanded of Israel in later centuries in the words: "The fear of the LORD is the beginning of knowledge" (Prov. 1:7). So declares Moses, their witlessness means they are living lives of no discernment, sanity, profundity, or objectivity. If only his people had the sense to profit from God's discipline then they might have grasped *why* and for what purpose he had chosen them as his elect. Isaiah 29:14 is based on this verse, and Paul bases his call to his Corinthian congregation (1 Cor. 1:18-19) on it. Paul declares that the wisdom of God is quite other than that which the world counts as wisdom, for the wisdom of God actually takes up into God's experience the pain and suffering (e.g., the Cross) of his people and uses it for his purposes of redemption. Such wisdom then is "the power of God."

> v. 30 How could one have routed a thousand,
>   and two put a myriad to flight,
>   unless their Rock had sold them,
>   the LORD had given them up?

Now comes that wisdom which Israel could neither grasp nor understand. In the normal course of events the Israelites might have won even an occasional battle by their own strength. But something was evidently far wrong with their relationship to Yahweh if just one enemy warrior could terrorize a thousand Israelites, and two (in poetic parallelism) could put ten thousand to flight. Being poetry, the figures for the enemy and for Israel are necessarily poetic exaggerations, but Moses uses exaggeration to make a point. He is not referring here to any historic occasion, but is making a general theological statement, that "If God be for us, who can be against us?" Moses had reached the basic recognition, upon which later writers could and did actually build, that God experiences the agony of having to execute both justice and mercy at the same time. God's way out of the impasse he has produced for himself is to decide, not to annihilate but to discipline his people, and to reveal to them that if they should rely upon their own strength alone they would undoubtedly be defeated in life. The people of God must find for themselves, prove the truth of the discovery to themselves as the Jewish sage Nachmanides puts it, that their defeat has come from God.

"Unless their Rock had sold them" implies God's having sold them out, as in Judg. 2:14; 3:8; 4:2, 9; 10:7; 1 Sam. 12:9; Ezek. 30:12; Ps. 44:14. This theme runs throughout the OT, the paradigm being this verse in the Song of Moses. Each defeat Israel sustained was an act of . . . *their* Rock! In other words, at no point in their history did God ever abandon his people. Even in defeat he remained, it would seem, "our" Rock, in his loyalty to the Covenant he had given to his own people, and in his consistent loyalty to his own name. For as we recognize, a rock does not change. It is the same yesterday, today, and forever. God has a purpose in allowing his people to meet with defeat. The modern idea that "God hates our sins, but loves us sinners" depends upon a Greek philosophical view of human nature. From Moses onward we see that, since there is no such "thing" as sin (there being only persons sinning, that is, sinners), it is sinners whom God has to punish and whom he has to chasten. That is why Paul must use the startling expression "He made him to be sin who knew no sin" (2 Cor. 5:21). To that end God may have to use force, to employ one "soldier of the LORD" to put a thousand to flight. "One of you puts to flight a thousand, since it is the LORD your God who fights for you, as he promised you" (Josh. 23:10; Lev. 26:8). Quoting this passage Isa. 30:17 can declare, "A thousand shall flee at the threat of one . . . therefore the LORD waits to be gracious to you. . . . For the LORD is a God of justice; blessed are all those who wait for him."

A God of justice . . . Actually, we noted, Israel's Rock had sold them (*makar*). This verb implies a tit-for-tat payment, a transaction such as only Yahweh could perform, or total justice, an eye for an eye. But by the same token *therefore* Yahweh waits to be gracious to you. What a tension this judgment suggests God must know in the greatness of his covenant love, his *hesed*. And what an amazing and deeply loving God this is to whom Moses introduces us. Clearly, the pathos of the poet is presented as the pathos of God.

Israel, the people of God, was known to Moses as the "host of the Lord" ("host" is the KJV word for "army"). Exodus 12:41-42 records a turning point in the "history" of Yahweh. "It was a night of watching by the Lord" (RSV, using a unique term to emphasize the uniqueness of the occasion) to bring them out of the land of Egypt. "On that very day, all the hosts of the Lord went out from the land of Egypt" (RSV), a fighting band with the Lord in their midst, truly an eschatological moment. God's host on earth was revealing the reality of God's host in the heavens (1 Kgs. 22:19), whom God employed in his war against the powers of evil. Yahweh is the God of battles and of victory (Exod. 15:1-18, 21). He is still the Rock that never changes. Accordingly because of the ultimate victory of Christ on the Cross, today's people of God are still called to take up their cross and fight the battles of the Lord. They are not the army of the saved. They are the army of the saving, or the "salvation army!"

Why does God allow wars to continue, people ask even today. They do so only because they have not recognized the answer to their cry in the theology of Moses. The NT is wiser than they. It does not deal with the issue, since it recognizes that Moses has given us the answer for all time in this his "Song of Moses."

v. 31   Indeed their rock is not like our Rock;
  our enemies are fools.

Who then are Israel's enemies? The gods of the peoples! And the peoples are one with their gods, since these Gentiles have created their gods in their own image. So gods and peoples as one confess together that they are "our enemies." Rather than the RSV's "For" *(ki)*, we might translate by the astonished exclamation: "Look how their rock is not like our Rock," when the "enemies" admit that their gods are no match for Israel's God (Exod. 14:25; Num. 23–24; so too in the experience of later generations, Josh. 2:9-11, etc.). This is an encouraging statement in Moses' sermon, one that is meant to bring his people back to faith. These enemies were their own "judges" (RSV; *pelilim*); they had become "arbitrators" of their own situation. As such they had become "fools" (NRSV).

The implication here is that the gentile people had an insight into the ways of Israel's God that Israel not only lacked — even though they had received a special revelation at Sinai — but against which they actually kicked. Does this mean that at least some gentile nations, like Nineveh in the book of Jonah, are more ready to hear the good news of God than we think? Unfortunately the LXX misses the point of this verse entirely by translating: "Our enemies being unintelligent." So too the NJB alters the text to read "Our enemies cannot pray for us." Each of these Versions is employing *eisegesis*, a reading into Moses' Hebrew of our human preconceptions of what we feel we ought to find in the text. But it is Moses we are listening to, not our own ideas. He wants us to discover that Israel's God alone has a purpose working out in history, one that includes even the chastisement of his own people.

vv. 32-33　　Their vine comes from the vinestock of Sodom,
　　　　　　　　from the vineyards of Gomorrah;
　　　　　　their grapes are grapes of poison,
　　　　　　　　their clusters are bitter;
　　　　　　their wine is the poison of serpents,
　　　　　　　　the cruel venom of asps.

As the author Jonathan Swift wrote, "Men have just enough religion to hate each other, but not enough for love." The extraordinary thing then is that it was just such creatively evil people whom God chose to chastise and educate. Yet says Moses on behalf of this perverse people, "our Rock" is LORD of all creation, including all the gods of the nations. Truly as LORD of all he can actually employ the evil in the world to serve the good. He can even work for the redemption both of Israel and, through Israel, of the nations of mankind.

As we see from the figure of the vine, evil is actually enfleshed in Israel's foes. The vine of Sodom, physically speaking, grew in a land of bitumen pits (Gen. 14:10). Morally speaking, our verse signifies the appalling degradation of Sodom's human inhabitants (Gen. 19:1-14; Ezek. 16:44-63; at Isa. 1:10 the prophet possibly takes for granted that his hearers would know his reference to Moses' Song). Evil is not a mere sentiment or concept that human beings may or may not entertain in their mind at will, as we have emphasized before. Evil is not something that exists apart from those who entertain it. Evil persons are pictured as being rooted in the poisonous vine, their cruelty to others who eat of their fruit coming from their having freely chosen to propagate this vine. For this reason God must punish not the sin, but the sinner. Consequently Israel must suffer in both body and "soul." The concept of "soul" is not found in the OT. As distinct from the philosophy of the Greeks, humans do not "have" a soul. A human being is a "living nephesh" (Gen. 2:7), a unified person living in union with other persons. As Targum Onkelos interprets here: "So shall be the bitter cups of the curse which they are to drink in the day of punishment" (cf. Jer. 25).

This understanding of evil is furthered when we look at the word for "serpents" (tanninim), which we find also at Gen. 1:21: "So God created the great sea-monsters." These were variously pictured as serpents (sea-serpents?), dragons, big fish (cf. Jonah), or as the indescribable inhabitants of the "waters under the earth" (Exod. 20:4). The tanninim were thus mythical representatives of evil and even of chaos itself. We recall Jesus' denunciation of a group of self-righteous upholders of the Law:

99

"You are from your father the devil" (John 8:44). Such is one of the "hard sayings" of Jesus, "hard" only to those who set aside the theology of Moses.

The figure of a vine is one that was employed to describe Israel over the centuries. Psalm 80:8-13 makes extensive use of it, probably having in mind Isaiah's parable at Isa. 5:1-7. John's Gospel thereupon carries forward the symbolism even farther (John 15:1-8). The argument here, of course, is that you become like what you worship. If you worship money you become covetous, if you worship power you become dictatorial. If you place your faith in the gods of Sodom and Gomorrah, then you become like them, vicious and lascivious.

The thin line that exists between good and evil is as sharp as a knife-edge. The vine produces what can be a good and wholesome fruit. The vineyard can be the place, especially at the grape harvest, of joyful song and dance. But it can also be the place of sheer eroticism and of drunkenness, such as we see connected with the worship of the gods of Canaan, Baal and Astarte, in Hos. 1–2. Thus it is that the joy of the LORD can so easily be transformed into "the cruel venom of asps." God's "pleasant planting" (Isa. 5:7) can at any time come under the judgment of his wrath.

In its efforts to emphasize that it is only the Gentiles who are "the sons of darkness" and that Israel alone are "the sons of light," the Dead Sea Scrolls Damascus Document 8:9 quotes this verse verbatim, and then adds: "of whom God said in Deuteronomy, 'the serpents are the kings of the peoples, and their wine is their ways; and the poison (or 'head') of asps is the "head" of the kings of Javan (Greece) who came to wreak vengeance on them.'" How truly this comment reveals that the Qumran community had strayed far from understanding God's revelation as it was given to their ancestors through Moses.

v. 34 Is not this laid up in store with me,
       sealed up in my treasuries?

100

We note that this is still a speech of God. An Eastern monarch, such as the pharaohs of Egypt with whom Moses was acquainted, possessed vast storehouses in which they kept their many treasures. These would be well and truly guarded and held under lock and key. In this sense God declares that he keeps the wickednesses of humanity in his storehouse on the door of which there is a seal. The meaning of the verb "laid up" *(kamas)* can only be guessed at, as it occurs only here. What we have is probably the form of the verb that was used in Moses' day; in later Classical Hebrew it became *kanas.* The sealing emphasized that the store was unopenable — by humans. Only God could break the seal (cf. Rev. 7:2). Humanity cannot redeem itself. This breaking of the seal will not take place until "that day," as later prophets declared, which will be "the day of vengeance of our God" (Isa. 61:2).

Yet we are to note that if God were to forsake Israel entirely, then the world would be delivered over to darkness. God has chosen to use Israel. Even when Israel rejects God and turns to the worship of self and to the idols that are created in the image of self, God will not give up using Israel — and thereby using evil — to create the good (Isa. 45:6-7). Evil is not merely the absence of God. As Carl Jung remarked, "One can hardly explain Auschwitz as merely an absence of good!" Nor, we might add, can we merely brush aside the concept of hell. All this immensity of evil — some of it now incarnate in the chosen people — actually has a place, a meaning. It is all stored up in God's treasury of purpose. Consequently since Israel is involved in the reign of evil, the NJB may well be correct in translating our verse "But he, is he not safe with me?," "he" being Yahweh's "treasured possession," his *segullah* mentioned at Exod. 19:5. God will continue to treasure his people even when (as in Deut. 32:35) "their foot shall slip." It is exactly then that he will "have compassion" on them (as in v. 36).

As Johannes Baptist Metz interprets Moses, this sealing up reveals to us a God who is "not 'above us' but 'before us,'" a God whose "transcendence reveals itself as our 'absolute future'" (*Theology of the World*, 88-89). It is grace that gives history its forward thrust, and this constitutes the basis of the Church's hope.

v. 35 Vengeance is mine, and recompense,
for the time when their foot shall slip;
because the day of their calamity is at hand,
their doom comes swiftly.

This verse is still the words of God. "Vengeance is mine": vengeance stored in *my* storehouse where it is completely sealed in. No human can open it. For no person knows the secrets of the human heart. Consequently no man or woman or child may take vengeance on others on his or her own initiative; for all human beings are sinners, including even the chosen people! God alone knows all, consequently to God alone belongs vengeance.

At this point, however, we must look more deeply at the word *naqam*, translated here by "vengeance." If we examine its uses elsewhere we come to the conclusion that it is better rendered by "vindication," for God's action may show itself either as punishment or as salvation, or as both at the same time!

Parallel with the noun *naqam* is another noun, *shillem*, translated in the NRSV by "recompense." First we note that, as a noun, it is a *hapax legomenon,* that is, it occurs only here. Its verbal root, however, means "to be complete." It is possible — and indeed probable — that the Masoretes (the Jewish editors of the text in later centuries, after the invention of the vowel system) read this word not as a noun at all but as a verb in the piel. It would then mean "and he makes complete." So the idea of completion or wholeness or fulfillment is expressed in parallel with the idea of "recompense" or "vindication."

Our verse is quoted at Isa. 34:8, where the noun *shillem* is written as *shillumim,* obviously the same term but now written as a plural. The same is true at Isa. 59:18, where the term appears as a verb and is rendered by "repay" in the NRSV. It is translated into Greek as *ekdikesis* at Luke 18:7 (RSV "vindicate"; NRSV

102

"justice"). At Jer. 51:56 it means "to reward, recompense, repay," in a neutral sense. In all it would appear that *shillem* is used here on the basis that Yahweh is Rock, in that God is utterly consistent, reliable, faithful to that purpose of his which the term *shillem* seeks to describe.

There is still another possibility, however, one that would be meaningful to Hebrew ears. That is to understand *shillem* to mean "and he creates *shalom*" ("peace," "wholeness," "welfare"). The modern critical scholar may reject this interpretation on the ground that the text presents us with a parallel which we ought not to disturb. Yet Hebrew poesy, as in the case of the Arabian poets, all throughout the OT delighted to find two or even more meanings to a word. So it is not for us to dispute the Hebrews' interest in this regard just because our poetic structure is different from theirs.

If the second possible reading of *shillem* we have noted carries in it any degree of likelihood, then we have a hint of Moses' later theological declaration, that God's "completion" of his handling of human sin is in reality the creation of peace, wholeness, salvation.

Paul quotes this verse at Rom. 12:19. (It is also to be found at Heb. 10:30.) Paul says two things: (1) we are not to take vengeance into our own hands. Only God may do so. (2) We are to "repay" good for evil. Paul's word is *antapodoso*, "I will repay," quoting exactly the LXX rendering of *shillem*. Then we in our turn are to repay by "creating *shalom*," by feeding our enemy instead of killing him, in fact by creating a state of loving-kindness between our enemy and us such as is the mark of God's *shalom*. Thus Paul did not invent this idea; he found it here in the Song of Moses.

It is the LXX term for "revenge," *ekdikesis*, that decides the NT usage. To this Paul adds the Greek pronoun *ego*, thereby seeking to emphasize that God's revenge is something utterly distinct from mankind's, for God's idea of revenge is to bring good out of evil, love out of hate.

The second line of Deut. 32:35, "because the day . . ." begins

103

with the little word *ki*. As well as "for" it can mean "that," as we have noted, following an unspoken verb. We might render it, "See how the day when their foot shall slip, how the day of their calamity, is at hand." This usage of "day" *(yom)* originated in its application to a battle that lasted one whole day, when either disaster or victory had to result. Moses' "specimen" battle, that between Israel and Amalek, ended when "the sun set" (Exod. 17:12). The great prophets learned this usage from Moses, and so spoke of "the day of the LORD" in these terms (e.g., Amos 5:18). Moreover, as we see it at Isa. 60:22, that "day" may be "predestined" *(atidhot)* and accomplished "quickly" *(hash)*. In a word, then, the meaning of the powers of evil, beyond our present human imagination, will remain hidden in God's store-house until the final day of calamity and doom arrives. Then all will be made plain in terms of a loving providence and of the ultimate compassion of God.

Although predestined the calamity will come about through Israel's free choice to go the wrong road, "when their foot shall slip," meaning meet with "a reverse of fortune" (S. R. Driver, *Deuteronomy,* 374). How kind to call Israel's apostasy just a slip of the foot! But then Moses' poem is about the grace of God and not about mankind. The Targum forgets this when it interprets "when their foot shall move to the captivity." This weakness of the Targum becomes a warning to the modern reader not to play down the centrality of grace in the teaching of Moses.

" 'The day' of their calamity is 'at hand' (Heb. 'near'), their doom comes swiftly." We are always to remember that what Jesus has to say is the fulfillment of what Moses and the prophets had to say. The Gospel of Mark is full of a sense of urgency, shown by its employing the word "immediately" several times even in its first chapter. In this way we watch the kingdom of God pressing in upon events. Thus as part of Jesus' message we hear "The kingdom of God 'is at hand' " (Mark 1:15). The kingdom was present in Jesus; it was revealed in the preaching of the Word; it was always *there,* for the eternal grace is always pressing in upon the time experience of humanity. It was the *aharit* which we have discussed before, the back of the coin, the eternal meaning and significance of the present moment, of the present event. This is what "at hand" meant to Moses. In their apostasy from God the people of God were already experiencing the significance of what they were doing. It was "at hand"; "the impending things" (*'atidot;* NRSV "doom") were coming "swiftly" into their awareness and experience, the things pre-pared for them in the divine plan. "The other side of the coin" was now being revealed, and it was turning out to be *revelation* of supreme grace and love. God's plan for Israel, which his people had rejected, declares Deutero-Isaiah (Isa. 48:18), was that "your prosperity would have been like a river." But God waits. It is only when Israel is at its lowest that God acts to redeem. God waits until Israel finally *sees* that the false gods are powerless, before he acts in judgment. So Moses' Song reveals to us a persistence of grace and retribution as an instrument of saving mercy.

"For the time when . . ." is thus not a reference to a chrono-logical hour. It is not so much *chronos* as it is *kairos,* God's chosen "moment," even as Jesus used the Greek word *hora* ("hour") at the wedding in Cana of Galilee (John 2:4).

It is held by many today in believing circles that the world is growing ever more evil, yet at the same time that God is waiting until humanity's foot has finally slipped before he in-tervenes. But God's intervention is one of salvation *in* destruc-tion. The valley of Achor (Hos. 2:15) is where Israel committed the ultimate act of disobedience to God (Josh. 7:24, 26). Still the prophet Hosea could dare declare that this place of Israel's failure was in reality "a door of hope." Such then is Moses' understanding of the unspeakable mercy of God.

v. 36   Indeed the Lord will vindicate his people,
     have compassion on his servants,
   when he sees that their power is gone,
     neither bond nor free remaining.

This sudden declaration about the compassion of God is quite fantastic. It is taken almost for granted today that mankind has always created its gods. "Fantastic" then is hardly a strong enough word in this case — fantastic to suppose that sinful Israel could ever have created the God of Moses. We have now learned that the demonstrations both of God's love and of his threatened punishments have not been able to persuade his people to turn toward God for any length of time (cf. Hos. 11:1-7). Thus when the final judgment seems inevitable, it is *at that point* that God says, "I will have compassion on my servants." This is the "only ever" God who is always willing to alter his course. As Hans Walter Wolff points out, God (in Hos. 11:8) "first reprimands himself! 'How could I?'" (*Anthropology of the OT,* 58). And as we learn from Paul at Rom. 5:8, seeing the Law of Moses to be fulfilled in Christ, he can then declare, "*While we still were sinners* Christ died for us."

There are those who hold to the theory of double predestination on God's part. They believe that God decides to save or to reject according to his own inscrutable will. Those who think in this fashion forget that God is not bound by his own decision to predestinate himself to be consistent, since God manifests himself as Rock whose will to save never changes. We have noted earlier that Moses does not use the noun *hesed* in his Song. It is only later prophets and psalmists, looking back over the centuries to Moses' day, who can recognize when hewing from this quarry that "steadfast love" is indeed the essential and unchanging activity of the God of the Covenant. God's *hesed* is describable today in the language of our culture in terms of the favorite hymn, "O Love That Will Not Let Me Go."

God can and does change his plan, as Moses shows here, for he is the "living God" (see Deut. 32:40 below). In *Die Reue Gottes* Jörg Jeremias shows that "divine repentance means that the God of love makes a decision to rescue his people from the judgment that he had first determined to bring upon them." That judgment, heard at vv. 22-25, was expressed no doubt in stereotypical and hyperbolic language. We have noted already how, as Walter Brueggemann puts it, "its massive, relentless force is necessary to penetrate the complacent self-assurance" of Israel "that 'it can't happen here,'" in a situation that was much the same in Jeremiah's day as here (*To Pluck Up, To Tear Down*, 169). So what the Song tells us is that God's final answer, despite the wars and famines and rebellious activities of his servants, is an answer of love. Our Song shows that, in his wisdom, God withholds his compassion until his people eventually find themselves wallowing helplessly in the depths into which God has necessarily cast them: "Their power is gone." "Bond" here may well mean "bound" — in the prisonhouse they have constructed around themselves. God's compassion falls equally on the "righteous" and on the self-centered egotist.

In light of this "theological" understanding of Moses' words, therefore, we would be wrong to limit the Hebrew terms *naqam* and *shillem* (used in v. 35) to a legal setting. This happened when a royal judge, such as the suzerain in the case of a covenant treaty (as scholars have shown us was the custom between nations in those days), makes decisions to condemn those who rebel against him and who refuse to acknowledge his sovereignty. He would then assume the form of warrior to assure justice (G. Ernest Wright, "The Lawsuit of God," 57). Rather God saw in Jeshurun the apostate what he really was, namely the son of God, because God looked upon him in compassionate understanding (Exod. 4:22).

Here then we reach a climax in the Song. ("In truth," *ki*) Yahweh will vindicate ("give vengeance!" Deut. 32:35) his people. Now the word for "people" has reverted to *'am*, the singular noun used throughout the OT for Israel almost exclusively. We recall that at v. 28 God had been forced to call them a mere *goi*, and so on a par with the Gentiles. This "vengeance" is the ultimate and final act of God's re-creative love.

God is judge. As such God dispenses absolute justice (cf. v. 4, "All his ways are just"). We should note that there is no word here in the Hebrew for "will vindicate," as the NRSV reads. According to the MT, "Yahweh will judge his people." Clearly we are meant still to hold before our eyes the idea of "revenge." On the other hand God remains faithful and loyal to his covenanted people. God cannot and will not let them go. So the next verb "have compassion" occurs in the hithpael, the subjective form of *naham*. Yahweh's empathy with his people leads him to "relent" rather than to "repent." This subjective form of the verb reveals that Yahweh "comforts himself," "eases himself." That is, God eases the tension within himself (cf. Hos. 11:8) — not by taking vengeance, but by having compassion. (See Friedemann Golka's exegesis of this word, George A. F. Knight and Golka, *Revelation of God*, 112).

It is interesting to note that Moses' petition to God in Exod. 32:12b corresponds almost exactly to the account of the hearing of his prayer in v. 14: "And the LORD changed his mind about the disaster that he planned to bring on his people." After all, we can hear Moses saying, the people of Israel are God's servants. That is actually what Israel is chosen to be — servants of the Covenant. Moses himself "served" God in this way. More than once, according to the Wilderness saga, God is heard threatening to wipe out rebellious Israel altogether and to start all over again, but this time with but one man, Moses. But each time this happens Moses himself persuades God to persevere (Exod. 32:7-14; Num. 11:29; Donald E. Gowan, *From Eden to Babel*, 101). How far in spirit this is from the Jerusalem Targum, which comments, "He comforts his righteous (sic!) servants."

Thus we are led step by step to learn that grace always prevails. For example, when the Flood was at its height we read, "But God remembered Noah" (Gen. 8:1). Such grace has continued to be revealed throughout both Testaments, Moses being the first to comment on it.

Here then we have a revelation, from the mouth of the LORD himself, that God's justice *is* his mercy, and nothing less. Isaiah 30:18 follows Moses in this memorable verse:

Therefore the LORD waits to be gracious to you;
therefore he will rise up to show mercy to you.

> For the LORD is a God of justice;
> blessed are all those who wait for him.

Moreover, as Paul says at 1 Cor. 2:7, many centuries after Moses' day, "We speak God's wisdom, secret and hidden, which God decreed before the ages for *our* glory." In other words, God's secret was made known at various moments throughout history, through revelation only, and especially now in Christ.

It is an aspect of his total justice that God does not keep on intervening in the life of sinful Israel, forever putting things right on Israel's behalf. God waits until his servants wallow in the effects of their own stupidity and wretched disloyalty. It is only when God sees that their power has gone, only when they are down at their lowest ebb, that he acts to show compassion upon them. For it is only then that human beings become aware that he is indeed the compassionate God and not the fussily interfering God (see Choan-Seng Song, *The Compassionate God*). The phrase "neither bond nor free remaining" seems to mean just this. Job 12:16 seems to paraphrase this phrase, "The deceived and the deceiver are his"; this refers to all extremes of Job's acquaintances, for all are sinners.

"Their power (literally, 'their hand,' meaning their competence, their support, something more material than spiritual) is gone." Curiously, this verb *azelat* is not Hebrew but Aramaic. Naphtali H. Tur-Sinai works from the supposition that the Song comes from the period of the formulation of the whole book of Deuteronomy and so suggests that this verb is a deliberate archaism (David A. Robertson, *Linguistic Evidence in Dating Early Hebrew Poetry*). Yet why should only one verb out of the whole poem be so? But if the Song is original to Moses, or was sung from generation to generation till it was penned in the eleventh century, then the problem disappears.

Moses had been brought up and educated in Egypt. There at the court he had learned the significance of the eighty or more gods whom the Egyptian people worshipped. Notably he had not been seduced to include any of these in his staunchly monotheistic faith (Deut. 32:16-17). (Now that we need no longer argue that our Song is a seventh-sixth century contrived work "in the manner of" Moses, the arguments whether or not Moses was a monotheist fall.) The Egyptians were equally certain that they knew all about what happened to the human soul, at least of royalty, after death. Their Book of the Dead is a detailed guide to life beyond the grave. Plato in his *Phaedo* (ca. 400 B.C.) taught the concept of the separation of the body and soul, and of the soul continuing on in an afterlife beyond death. He had learned this from the even then ancient Egyptians, whom he greatly admired. This belief is to be found virtually universally both throughout history and today, and is basic to all the theories of transmigration of the soul held in most of the religions of the East, including Japan. Israel is completely unique in having no such theories about the afterlife. Moses, who put his stamp on Israel's faith, shows not a trace of such a belief in the immortality of the "soul." In Israelite thought a human being is one entity, a single *nephesh;* this means therefore that when a person dies, all of the person dies, and his or her end is that of the grave — the deceased is gathered to his ancestors in their graves. Neither Moses nor any of the prophets reveals that they possess any mythology of death of any kind. Their ideas on Sheol, which simply meant the grave, reveal their awareness of a mere popular belief learned from the Canaanites, that the dead "semi-exist" below the ground as mere shadows ("shades") of whole persons. On the other hand all thoughtful Israelites believed that, following upon the uniqueness of Yahweh, Yahweh had in his hand the complete disposal of life and death. Since a human person, male or female, is created in the image of God, the whole of his or her life must necessarily possess eschatological significance.

Accordingly God waits to rescue his people until his nation is *in extremis.* But when he acts he acts indeed! So we note that God uses time, which is part of what he has created (cf. Exod. 34:6, "slow to anger"; Isa. 48:19; Ezek. 20:22). God waits. And God waits in agony of heart, until *his* moment of vengeance arrives. It is only then that God passes judgment (not "vindicates," NRSV), and it is that judgment which is so fantastic. Before our eyes we see a militant God, theologically understood, yielding to be a God of compassion. God's "work" is to deal with the whole "eschatologically conditioned" people of Israel and save them as they are, body-soul-spirit persons. As Ezek. 37 puts it, looking back to Moses' teaching, God may take the "dry bones" of his people and breathe life into them again . . . and again . . . and again. On each occasion God waits until Israel is "a nothing" (cf. Deut. 32:10), nonbeing *(tohu),* for only then will stupid Israel recognize that the dead cannot raise themselves from death (Jer. 30:12-17).

We might even postulate at this point that, since the Song of Moses is that quarry out of which so much later theology was hewn, the view of the great prophets about a theology of the creation of the universe *ex nihilo* arose from their discovery that God had recreated Israel too *ex nihilo.* The human mind cannot comprehend the meaning of "nothing" without their being "something" to compare it with. Redeemed Israel was indeed "something" to rejoice over, and so was in itself a proof that there was a creator God. Here a "good" had indeed emerged from an "evil." But evil, as Irenaeus put it, can only emerge out of some good, so that the originator of the succession can only be a good God.

Later generations claimed Moses as a prophet even as did Jesus (Luke 16:29, 31). How are we to understand this designation of Moses in relation to the depth of meaning of this verse?

According to Alan Richardson, "If we think of prophecy as primarily the discernment of the underlying purpose of contemporary events, which carries with it an insight into the pattern and goal of history . . . we shall understand that the fulfilment of prophecy means the corroboration by later historical happenings of the prophetic foreshadowings of the truth, the typological fulfilment . . . of patterns that have been given in the earlier stages of Israel's history" *(Christian Apologetics).* In other words, God's "foreknowledge" is not the kind of absoluteness usually attached to the notion of God. God remains free, for his Word is now incorporated in his prophet; it is the latter who is now empowered to embody the Word in his own life and faith — and the human prophet is very vulnerable flesh.

At Deut. 32:18 we saw how Moses recognized that holiness was the one absolute attribute of the living God. Now we discover that he reveals the other and second absolute attribute of God, which is love. Just as God's holiness is beyond human imagination, so is his love. This surely is a topic whose reality grows in the hearts of Israel out of Moses' prophetic proclamation until 1 John 4:16 can state with confidence that "God is love." "Their power is gone," then. But that only means that God longs to lead his people into a new source of power, the power of his own holy love. The last three verses of the book of Micah, reflecting our v. 36, are an exclamation of wonder and joy at the reality of the redeeming love of God (Mic. 7:18-20).

Friedrich Baumgartel writes: "The OT Word is to be understood as gospel; it is powerful for us, the active power of God for us . . . in the evangelical knowledge through faith that the fundamental promise of the old covenant has become realized in Jesus Christ is anchored in the affinity of the Christian faith to the OT Word" ("The Hermeneutical Problem of the Old Testament," 151-52).

But then is this Song of Moses, as it deals with the apostasy of Israel and then with God's compassion on his servants, really history? Does it handle "historical fact?" Gerhard von Rad applies himself to this issue: "Only where Yahweh had revealed himself with his deeds and his word was there history for Israel. And at this point the conflict with the modern view of history was bound to arise, sooner or later. For the modern view is perfectly capable of drawing a picture of history without God" (quoted from Jasper Høgenhaven, *Problems and Prospects of OT Theology*, 60; cf. von Rad, *OT Theology*, 2:418). Surely the OT in general, and Moses in particular, must be allowed to speak for themselves out of their contextual witness to the covenantal experience in which they lived, moved, and had their being.

Accordingly we today must accept the historical fact that the OT was the Bible of the early Church for the whole first century of Christianity, and that the statement in 2 Tim. 3:16-17 applies only to the OT, in that the NT had not been written at that point in time.

It is "on his servants," then, that God has compassion. As James A. Carpenter suggests in the spirit of this verse in the Song, "Perhaps Christianity, following Jesus, should not seek to establish itself as anything except servant, should not seek its own but should give itself for the life of the world, witnessing always to the one absolute to which he witnessed, the absolute love of God" (*Nature and Grace*, 71).

A person living — or merely existing — without awareness of the compassionate love and forgiveness of God supposes that his or her "religion," whatever it may be, is his glory — unless he becomes disillusioned with his religion. Then that person recognizes his lost ideals and grows weary with a sense of the meaninglessness of his life. Not knowing that love is of God, a person believes that "love" is something like maintaining the status quo of his or her own ideas, unaware that it is evil that disturbs him. So G. Ernest Wright remarks, "The search for safety, contentment and happiness," offered to us today by a host of human sects and 'isms' — "life without conflicts within and without," as the Eastern religions offer, "must for so many Christians have become the solid goals of Christian 'love'" (*The OT and Theology*, 94). This is a dangerous illusion, as Moses shows us here, even as he reveals to us the very nature of the living God.

vv. 37-38   Then he will say: Where are their gods,
        the rock in which they took refuge,
    who ate the fat of their sacrifices,
        and drank the wine of their libations?
    Let them rise up and help you,
        let them be your protection!

So Yahweh is the God of both judgment and of redeeming love, the God who bears Israel's sins on his own heart because he has judged the rebellious behavior of his servant and so has felt the enormity of their apostasy. It is Yahweh who thereby rescues them when they are actually at their lowest, when at last their "power" — their egotistical belief in their own strength and purpose — "is gone."

It is at this point then that Yahweh asks Israel a question, as he does to Adam in the garden. "Where are their gods" now — those who ate the fat of Israel's sacrifices, who drank the wine of Israel's drink offering? For they have totally failed to respond to Israel's cry (cf. Judg. 10:14), totally failed to be their protection, though Israel fled to them for protection (Isa. 43:11)! Moreover, it is a case of "like god, like worshipper." Israel cannot help itself, for its gods, being "no-gods," cannot help anyone. So God invites Israel to see their need. They no longer possess a "refuge" *(sitrah)*, a shelter from the storm.

Every sacrifice not offered to the living God is automatically thereby dedicated to demons, because demons are "nonbeings." The cup of demons is the cup from which a drink offering is made to a deity at either private or public meals or on similar festive occasions. Such an act was thus a blasphemous saying of "grace before meals." Paul was aware of the content of this verse when he gave his forthright warning at 1 Cor. 11:27-28 about eating and drinking the cup of the Lord unworthily and so of being guilty of profaning the body and blood of the Lord. He would have had the text of the LXX before him as he penned those words. The LXX alters the original "their sacrifices" and "their libations" to "your . . ." in each case. Once again we meet with the forceful *argumentum ad hominem* that Moses has used before in his Song.

The God of the Bible is the same yesterday, today, and forever. The God of Paul and the Father of Christ is therefore the same God as the God of Moses. Consequently we see how the interpretation of the Cross, given us theologically in the NT and based on these verses, understands the risen Christ in terms of the title that some have given him, "Christus Victor." Moreover, to believe "in" the Cross is to take upon ourselves the cross of Christ as our own, and so to allow ourselves to be crucified with Christ. Israel of old is here called upon to accept into its own experience, *on behalf of others* (Exod. 19:5, as God's priests to the nations), what God in the pain of his heart has first done for Israel.

Where are their gods? According to G. Henton Davies, their disappearance leaves the way open for God, as we find in the next verse, to announce himself and to describe exactly who he is. First, Israel's own "hand" had failed them, their own power, their self-conceit; now the gods of the nations had failed Israel as well. Here we meet not with "religion," not with a philosophy of life, but with what some have called "auto-kerygma," the reality of God conveyed to Israel directly in the form of judgment for their sins. The very next verse is the vehicle of that revelation: "I . . ."

Patrick Skehan discovered a fragment of a Dead Sea Scroll covering vv. 37-43 of the Song of Moses. It differs considerably in places from the Hebrew text. In his discussion of the scroll Skehan demonstrates features in it in common with the LXX. But we may ignore Skehan's findings now that we feel sure of the Mosaic origin of our Song in the form it has come down to us. Thus as we noted at Deut. 32:8, at times the teaching of the Dead Sea Scrolls may be disregarded. Of great interest, however, is that the phraseology we find in the next verse is very akin to what we find in the Ugaritic texts!

v. 39　See now that I, even I, am he;
　　　　　there is no god beside me.
　　　　I kill and I make alive;
　　　　　I wound and I heal;
　　　　and no one can deliver from my hand.

Who then is this "god" Yahweh? the Lord GOD continues. Is he in reality the living God, the creator of the ends of the earth?

And does he indeed reveal himself to human beings? Moreover, what is the meaning of God's "being"? The answers to these questions sound forth now from the mouth of Yahweh himself, and they may be compared with two other self-utterances given to Moses to hear, at Exod. 3:7-15 and 34:6-7. We shall refer to these presently.

God begins his declaration to Moses with "See now," in the plural. God is addressing his people Israel, and through Israel the whole of the human race. The word means "employ a mental picture." "Now" (*'attah*) may well be understood to mean "at this instant," "at your moment in time." Then follows the particle *ki*. This little word can mean "that" after such a verb as "he said *(that)* . . ." But it can also indicate an impressive assertion, after such a verb as "I swear *(that)*. . . ." God's actual declaration then follows as three Hebrew words, *ani, ani, hu*: "I, I, He." That is all! Clearly these personal pronouns are words meant to express the concept of God the speaker as "person," of God as "living." There are various ways of taking them literally, however.

William F. Albright declares they mean "I am I," even adding "This translation is absolutely certain" ("Some Remarks on the Song of Moses in Deuteronomy xxxii," 342f.). On the contrary G. Ernest Wright, Albright's own student, later declared, "The *hû'* ('he') is surely not a divine name, but the common copulative pronoun" ("The Lawsuit of God," 32 n. 20). So Wright's rendering would be "I (alone) am the one."

Anyway these words surely declare that God is personal, the living God — in fact the only Reality as conceivable by human minds in personalized terms. Then follows, "There is (are) no god(s) beside me." Hebrew *elohim* is of course a plural noun. When used of false gods it is normally to be understood as a plural. But when used of Israel's God it may be both singular and plural at once, as at Gen. 1:26; Isa. 6:8, and elsewhere. (See my discussion of this vital issue in George A. F. Knight and Friedemann W. Golka, *Revelation of God*, 46ff.) Moreover, in this divine self-utterance God uses "trinitarian" language about himself: God is Creator, Savior, and Life-giver.

116

One thing wholly self-authenticating about what this verse reveals is that none of the gods, thought up and "created" by the human mind, could ever turn out to be like Yahweh. The human mind is unable to conceive of the living God, and can only think of God in pictures — as remarked above. So God has to summon the hearers of the poem to do more than hear: they are to "See!" Eberhard Jüngel expounds further that revelation is "not an other over against God" but "a reiteration of God." Revelation is that event in which the *being of God* itself comes to word. When we talk of revelation we are not talking of a something other than God; we are talking about the God who is constituted by this act of revelation. God is nevertheless free in this. "God's presence is always *God's decision to be present*" (*The Doctrine of the Trinity*, 19). God has being in loving.

Isa. 43:10, based upon our verse, reads: "That you may understand . . . that *ani hu* ('I, He')," or with Albright perhaps "I am I." It proceeds, "Before me no god *(el)* was formed; *anoki anoki YHWH* ('I, I, Yahweh'). . . ." (There is no verb "to be" as such in Hebrew.) "And besides me there is no savior," a declaration that links the "being" of God to his "being in loving" mankind (cf. Exod. 3:12). At Exod. 3:13 Moses asks God what his *name* is, to which comes the reply "I become *(ehyeh)*" ("with you," v. 12). This then is the name which Moses declares at Deut. 32:3 he will proclaim, in order to explain just what the "greatness of our God" really implies. And this revelation is given to one man, and to one man only, uniquely to the one who alone saw God "face to face" (Num. 12:6-8). This means it was not Moses' imagination or his "soul" or his heart that perceived, but the whole of his being, his *nephesh*.

We make three points here. First, the verb *ehyeh* ("I become") appears to be used as the first person equivalent of the third person, *Yahweh*, although the vowels used in this divine name raise questions that have been the occasion of much scholarly debate. For example, the much later scribe(s) whom we call P, writing at Exod. 6:2, seems to take for granted that the consonants *y-h-w-h* are the equivalent of *y-h-y-h*, and this may well be so. Second and consequently, Albright speculated that this form was in fact a hiphil of the verb *hayah* and so would be an active form, making it possible to understand the consonants YHWH to mean "he who brings into being, who creates." Third, however, the emphasis we must make is that this word, whether as verb or noun, expresses what we might call "relationship" between God and mankind, as in "I shall become *with* you" (Exod. 3:12) or, as the manner in which both the books of Hosea and Jonah begin, "The word of the LORD that *came to* . . ." *(hayah el)*.

The LXX, which was used so extensively by the early Church, translates "I AM" at Exod. 3:14 by *ho on* ("the being"). The translation was made in the 3rd cent. B.C. in the Hellenized city of Alexandria in Egypt, which was one of the chief centers of Greek philosophical study. However, the Hebrew ought not to be translated into English by "I AM," for that represents a mere philosophical idea such as Plato delighted to expound, one which sets aside the personal and lovingly concerned relationship between God and Israel that Moses rejoiced to expound and which had become known to him in terms of revelation.

This totally personal relationship is revealed when God declares that it is he who kills and who makes alive, who casts into Sheol and brings up again (Ps. 16:10; Matt. 10:28) and yet, even as he does so, that God is *present with* his child in Sheol (Ps. 139:8). This reality is formalized into the title Immanuel; this one English word is a whole phrase which means "God is *with* us" (Isa. 8:8; Matt. 1:23).

Since the living God of Deut. 32:39 is the God whom Moses knew as "I am he who becomes *with* you," mankind's life is therefore dependent upon God's "life." In the Exile, for example, when all around seemed to be "dead," God answers his prophet, "As I live, . . . I have no pleasure in the death of the wicked" (Ezek. 33:10-11). This answer then takes shape in Ezek. 37, in the parable of *God's* action in resurrecting his people in "the valley of the dry bones." This reality about God, beginning in

Deut. 32:37, is what each new generation from Moses' day till ours must discover and realize for itself.

The remainder of our verse describes God's nature in personal terms, in action in creative power. It is a false understanding of the biblical revelation to read into this verse that God's creativity proceeds in a smooth and orderly and developing manner. From the beginning this has never been so. It was *out of* chaos that God created light (Gen. 1:2-3). Isa. 45:5-7 can then declare, "I am Yahweh . . . I form light and create darkness; I make weal *(shalom)* and create woe (*ra*', 'evil')." The verbs used here are not synonyms. Light is of God himself, so he only needs to form it, fashion it, as a potter fashions clay that is already there to hand. But God must create *(bara')* darkness, for darkness is not "of" God at all. Similarly God "makes" weal *('asah shalom)*, for *shalom* is of himself. Yet God has to "create" *(bara')* evil, for evil is not "of" God. The verb *bara'*, as in Gen. 1:1, is used of God's actions alone, not mankind's. We can illustrate these usages from the experience of Moses, for *out of* Moses' dumbness God speaks forth his creative Word, *with* Moses' mouth (Exod. 4:11-12). God's actions in creation, then, are not describable in terms of a smooth progression, of a straight line from beginning to end, from birth to death, from the primitive to the advanced, from the primeval to the modern world. This basic assertion is quoted from the Song of Moses in the Song of Hannah (1 Sam. 2:6), which in its turn forms the basis of the Song of Mary (Luke 1:46-55).

All throughout the "progression" there have been present those (to us) inexplicable disruptions, such as we see in "nature red in tooth and claw" or in the dozen cycles of defeat and renewal portrayed in the book of Judges. As Paul puts it, "the whole creation has been growing in labor pains until now; and not only the creation, but we ourselves" (Rom. 8:22-23). Dinosaurs have arisen and disappeared, volcanoes have destroyed great areas of fertile land, yet only in order that new forms of life might emerge.

In the area of human experience Isa. 40–55, whose author

depends so much upon our Song, employs the verb *bara'* sixteen times to describe what God is doing with Israel — not creating so much as re-creating after destruction and disaster. One might say that the "final solution" of the Jewish people, to use Adolf Hitler's phrase, had been attempted in the year 587 B.C. when the Babylonian armies obliterated Jerusalem. In his prophecies Amos, two centuries before, had predicted that *the end* would come upon Jerusalem by the death that God's hand would deliver. But the author of the book of Lamentations, who lived through the debacle, knew the Song of Moses, and so could assert God's own words from Deut. 32:39, "I kill and I make alive; I wound and I heal." (See Robert Martin-Achard and S. Paul Re'emi, *God's People in Crisis*, which deliberately treats Amos and Lamentations together, in order to show the nature of God as Moses knew it.) In fact, in crisis after crisis the story of God's handling of his people advances through wounding and healing, death and resurrection (Ezek. 47) until we enter the revelation given to us in the NT (Acts 2:22).

So then God has to be cruel to be kind. As the Great Physician God has to use his knife, his scalpel, upon the diseased body of his chosen people. Blood, as the bearer of God's gift of life, must be shed before life can ensue. The scalpel may even be the sword in the hands of the heathen, as at Deut. 32:25. The gods cannot save from the powers of evil (v. 27), from cancer or from sin; and sin itself may be death to the human spirit (Prov. 7:27). Moses had himself experienced how Yahweh had chosen to kill Pharaoh's firstborn son and all the firstborn in the land of Egypt (Exod. 12:12) before God could bring his own firstborn son into the *shalom* revealed at Sinai (Exod. 4:23). Yahweh then "signs" the death warrant with the words *ani YHWH*. As Paul puts the issue at 1 Cor. 1:28, God has first to "reduce to *nothing*" (*katargein*) things that are before he can act creatively. So difficult is it for modern sophisticated men and women to grasp this truth that the KJV finds it necessary to translate this Greek verb in seventeen different ways.

Jeremiah again, depending on Deut. 32:39, classified those

who remained in Jerusalem when the Babylonian army was threatening to destroy the city as the "bad figs," even as he pointed to two baskets of figs set down before the temple of the LORD (Jer. 24). These "theologians" supposed that what God required of them was merely to "obey the Torah," yet they did not have a heart to "know that I am Yahweh." However, God had other plans for those whom Jeremiah called "the good figs." It transpired that these had to "walk through the fires" of the exile (Isa. 43:3), to suffer and to "die," yet thereafter to be reborn (Ezek. 36:26-27), to be resurrected to a new beginning. Jeremiah thus draws a picture in his parable of how the purposes of God are understandable only in terms of grace.

In Deut. 32:39 God speaks in the first person: "I." He is addressing Israel through Moses. "Why would God bother to speak to one who could not hear [i.e., his people]? Humanity is — more than trees or animals — uniquely the *recipient* of revelation" (Thomas C. Oden, *The Living God,* 24). Thus in being able to hear (to obey is another matter) Israel learned not *whether* God exists, but *who* God is, and what God's distinctive *character* is.

But stranger still, as we have noted before, at Isa. 45:14-15 God does not re-create Israel "from above." God is *in* Israel, as the KJV correctly translates the Hebrew, hiding himself in Israel's experience of life and death. God then was *in* his servant Jeshurun, the beloved (Deut. 32:15). No Israelite in consequence needed ever again to ask the very human question, "Where is God in all this?" For the answer came to them, we might say "existentially," in the words of their prophets, beginning (at Isa. 53:1, 4) with the question, "Who [could have] believed what we have heard? . . . Surely he has borne our griefs and carried our sorrows" (RSV).

This God, the creator of both life and death, was allowing himself to be smitten with disease and brought down to taste death in the experience of his servant Israel (Isa. 53:9-10; cf. 2 Cor. 5:19). For as the prophet of the exile put it squarely (Isa. 43:24b), "You (Israel) have made me the servant who bears your sins" (an alternative but legitimate translation to that in the NRSV). So-called Christian orthodoxy, if it builds its theology from the NT alone, finds it appalling to suggest that God knows what it is to die. But of course it is appalling because it is true, just as it is true that God — in Christ — tasted death on the Cross — and in Auschwitz.

Within the progression mentioned above there occur two "moments" of creative activity that move from death to life. The first is the Babylonian exile. Israel in exile in the Tigris-Euphrates Valley had eventually become a mere collection of dry bones, a fact known existentially to the prophet Ezekiel who was there, with them, in person. But "God was in Israel" when this happened to his people (cf. Isa. 45:14). The One who declares here that "I am he; I kill and I make alive" had by then allowed "his enemies" to do him down to death, *in* Israel — an amazing and fantastic reality. But being the living God ("as I live forever," Deut. 32:40) God could shrug off death and then raise to life — *with* himself (Immanuel, "God is *with* us") — his exiled people. "I . . . will cause flesh to come upon you (the completion of your *nephesh*, to render you whole persons once again), . . . and put breath in you (Heb. "spirit," *my* spirit; Ezek. 36:27), and you shall live; and you shall know that I am the LORD" (Ezek. 37:1-6).

The second "moment" in God's recreative activity took place when "God was in Christ" (2 Cor. 5:19 KJV), who died and was raised again as a whole person, and not as a spirit or a soul. This reality was brought home to the disciples when they "saw" the marks of the nails and the wound in Christ's side.

That, then, is the greatness of our God, to which Moses has summoned not only Israel — and therefore the Church — but all nations to ascribe to God (Deut. 32:3). His greatness is that as Almighty God, Creator of life and death, God himself entered into death in order that his beloved might be rescued from "the power of sin and death."

It is because God is LORD of life, then, that he can use death by entering into it himself to bring about resurrection into eternal life (*le-'olam*, "into eternity"). No other verse in the Song, therefore, so clearly reveals that God is the living God (cf. John 6:57). He is the "living Father" of the son, Jeshurun. Incidentally, we note also that, as Raymond E. Brown declares, the I AM statements of Jesus describe his relationship, not first to God but to mankind (*The Gospel according to John I-XII*, 434), in that they are filled with the potentiality of those very words heard by Moses at Exod. 3, and here in Moses' Song.

A final word is in order about the emptiness of much traditional interpretation of the Song, represented in Jeremiah's day by those whom he classed as the "bad figs" — the theologians who could only cry "The temple of the LORD," meaning "all we need is a national religion that maintains the status quo." A Targum on this verse reads, "I smote the house of Israel, and will heal them at the end of the days. Not even Gog and his armies, whom I have permitted to make war against them, can grab them out of my hand." The Jerusalem Targum limits God's action in redemption to the time beyond death: "I make alive the dead in the world to come." Modern piety follows the Targum at this point. Consequently it cannot understand what Jesus meant when he declared, "Let the dead bury their own dead" (Matt. 8:22; Luke 9:60). For if we live our life here and now in and with God, we remain *in* him beyond the grave.

Where now is the theologians' concept of the transcendence of God? What Moses does for us here is to show that transcendence has nothing to do with distance, with either space or time. According to Terence E. Fretheim (*The Living God*, 70), transcendence refers to "the way in which the Godness of God manifests itself in . . . 'relatedness' — for God a permanent state of affairs."

v. 40   For I lift up my hand to heaven,
and swear: As I live forever.

Since then this is what God is like, imparted to us by his own revelation of himself through the Word, God now swears in consequence that he will bring about "death" wherever it is deserved and wherever it can become the door to newness of life. "I declare that I have but to raise my hand to heaven (as a human being does in the taking of an oath, 'heaven' here being an expression for 'myself'), and I have but to say: (so we paraphrase) In accordance with *my* (very emphatic in the Hebrew) life, which is the same yesterday, today, and forever" (Heb. *le 'olam*, "into eternity"). It is therefore "of" his nature as the ever-living God that he must act in this life and death manner, one which is in conformity with the reality of eternity (T. C. Vriezen, *An Outline of OT Theology*, 186; W. Eichrodt, *Theology of the OT*, 2:24-25; Matt. 16:19; 25:34). We note then that the Word may be uttered either "from above" or "from below" (Exod. 33:11).

The LXX is careful to translate Heb. *hai* and *hayyim* ("life"), not by Gk. *bios*, which we might regard as the natural life force, but by *zoe*, a noun which well represents the power inherent in the Hebrew term, for it means life as such in itself. Moreover, God himself makes this differentiation clear, consistently and historically, at special moments in Israel's story (e.g., Isa. 44:24-28). Greek *zoe* is life that is independent of disease, suffering, and death. "I seriously doubt that a straight line can express the immense complexity of God's saving activity in the world. . . . It is such a handy tool for theologians to have. We have to concede that a straight line is one of the most basic and essential units for science and technology. . . . But . . . to turn God into a straight-line God is to caricature God" (Choan-Seng Song, *The Compassionate God*, 25). Love is not a geometrical concept. It is not a straight line. So Deut. 32:40 pursues the theme of v. 39. For mankind not to see this reality about God shows lack of "wisdom" *(hokmah)*, and that, says v. 6, is stupidity. Mankind is disdaining "the fear of the LORD" which is the beginning of wisdom, and to do that is no less than an offense against God. God is all-holy, so therefore God is the enemy of all evil and will destroy it to the death. But if that evil is incarnated in "living" children of God "who hate me" (v. 41), is God's holiness then finally vindicated in their obliteration? No, as Moses has already said at v. 36. Compassion and mercy win out in the soliloquy we are given to hear again and again in the OT taking place in God's heart. So it is interesting to note the meaning of the double "bands" some Christian ministers (and the British legal profession) wear along with their gowns. By this dual sign they exhibit that the gospel they preach is proclaimed in tension between judgment and salvation; if the wearer is a judge that person witnesses to the fact that ever since the days of Moses the tension lies between justice and mercy. The wearing of bands also reminds the judge that when one sat in judgment in Moses' day the judge's bench was known as *elohim* ("God"; Exod. 21:6; 22:8-9). This was because the judge had to execute the judgment-in-mercy, which is "of" the nature of God himself.

> v. 41   If I whet my flashing sword,
> and my hand takes hold on judgment;
> I will take vengeance on my adversaries,
> and will repay those who hate me.

Just as at Deut. 32:23 this is a threat, expressed in this case by the word "when," rather than NRSV "if," God could quite naturally "whet my flashing sword," for he is the God of justice or judgment. He is the warrior God, always at war with the powers of evil. God could un-create what he has first created. He could return the humanity he has created to nothing, to join the chaos that was there in the beginning. Jeremiah felt the possibility of this with a sense of horror (Jer. 4:23-26). "Unsheathing his flashing sword" speaks of God's judgment *going forth*, in other words acting within history. That such an action has eschatological significance is shown by the literal meaning of the Hebrew: "If I 'teeth' the 'lightning' of my sword," meaning sharpen it, give it teeth (see RSV mg).

Then follows an anthropomorphic picture of God acting

125

as a human being might act: "my hand takes hold on ('grasps') judgment" — that is, picks it up and uses it firmly and in actuality — then I would be " 'returning' vengeance on my enemies." The verb *shub* ("return") emphasizes that God would be rendering equal justice, exactly an eye for an eye, as we have heard before from Moses. God would not be avenging himself like a vengeful Eastern monarch who does not know when to stop his cruel activities in "pacifying" a subject people (cf. Isa. 10:5-11). Then God adds, "I . . . will repay those who hate *me*" — not *you*, not "Israel my people." "Repay" (*shillem;* RSV "requite") is the verb we examined at Deut. 32:35, where the NRSV translates "recompense."

At v. 35, just as here, *shillem* was coupled with the word *naqam*, "vengeance." We saw that the best sense of *naqam*, employed as a verb, is "vindicate." Thus what God actually says there is "Vindication is mine, and so is *shillem.*" We rendered *shillem* by the idea of making complete, whole, fulfilled, and even by "creating *shalom*" (creating peace, wholeness, welfare). We noted too that this is how Paul in his turn understood this active verb, for in quoting v. 35 at Rom. 12:19 he declares that we, following the actions of God, are to repay good for evil (v. 21). So in the words that Moses employs at Deut. 32:41, God will bring forth out of his total judgment the total gift of vindication and peace, acting within what Ezekiel calls God's "covenant of peace" (Ezek. 34:25).

"I will take vengeance on my adversaries," says God. God's war against evil is no abstract theological notion. Evil is incarnated in human beings, so God must wage war — not against evil but against evil-doers. But who are God's adversaries (Ps. 68:1)? Was it the Canaanites, who "hated" Yahweh? Or was it the Amalekites of Moses' own day? (Exod. 17:8-13). Over many centuries the Edomites seem to have acted so; as "cousins" of Israel, ever since the day that Esau lost the birthright of a blessing bearing "power" Israel and Edom were at war with each other. But the "prophetic" nature of Moses' Song leads us to recognize that God's enemies can arise at any time in history.

(For a vivid exposition of the basic evil in human nature that leads a whole nation to be God's enemy, see Mária Eszenyei Széles, *Wrath and Mercy;* and for the idea of a "master race," see Martin Hengel, *Jews, Greeks and Barbarians,* 56-57.)

"My adversaries," however, must in reality be the enemies of *my* people at any point in time. Since God is bound up with his people in covenantal love *(hesed),* those who fight against the people of God find themselves fighting against God. Those who war against the outworking of God's plan for the redemption of the gentile world, in and through Israel's obedience or even disobedience, find themselves actually fighting against God. In other words, therefore, God shares the pain of Israel's sufferings through the bonds of the Covenant. God does not remove the sufferings of his covenant people, as the modern agnostic thinks he ought to, if he is really God. Nor does God "stop the war," as many have prayed him to do. God shares the pain of it all by putting his own shoulder to the yoke alongside of us, his chosen people.

> v. 42   I will make my arrows drunk with blood,
>   and my sword shall devour flesh —
>   with the blood of the slain and the captives,
>   from the long-haired enemy.

God must necessarily pursue his just war, his war of judgment, relentlessly against the powers of evil. These powers, as we have recognized, may be represented in human beings of flesh and blood. In consequence of this reality God says, "I will *make* my (eschatological) arrows drunk with blood" (the life fluid of living creatures) — not just "let it happen" as a by-product of my judgment, but "*make* it happen." Again, "*my* (eschatological) sword shall devour *flesh*" — not ideas, philosophical systems, theologies, ideologies, or any other humanly conceived "-isms," but the flesh of *people*. God will bring forth justice through the blood, not only of those who are killed in battle, but also of those who, having been taken prisoners, are then slaughtered (cf. Isa. 7:1-2). This picture of carnage was used much by later prophets, a picture of "all hell let loose."

The final picture is that of warrior enemies of God ("those who hate me," Deut. 32:41) with flowing tresses of hair. What this means is difficult to determine. The word "long-haired" looks to be a feminine plural form of the name Pharaoh! Did Egyptian warriors, as representative of Israel's enemies in Moses' day, go into battle with long hair as a mark of being consecrated, like priests, to their bloody task? Morris S. Seale would translate by "enemy heads with dishevelled hair" on the grounds that nomadic warriors (such as the Amalekites?) fought in battle with their hair streaming behind them, uncut, as a mark of their dedication to their god (*The Desert Bible*, 28). To this day it is strongly taboo to touch the hair on the head of many Pacific Islanders. The LXX merely has "the heads of the enemies who rule over them." Thus it generalizes where it does not understand, and in so doing takes the sting out of this strange picture of ruthless nihilism.

The Versions may well have merely pietistically smoothed over the sting of the indictment about the enemy, on the ground that the phrase comes from God himself. However, "long-haired" may simply equal such an opprobrious utterance as "cotton-picking" or "bloody-minded," such as a modern speaker might employ today or just as Jesus did when he called King Herod "that fox" (Luke 13:32).

Yet what we are left with in our mind is a vision of the execution of justice to the uttermost, of the shedding of human blood which itself is of course holy to the LORD. That is what God must be like in himself as the God of all holiness who demands that his people be holy too (Exod. 19:6). We should note, moreover, that some of our Psalms are not afraid to quote the "bloody" language used here (cf. Ps. 68:21-23). They recognize that God's justice must not only be done — it must be seen to be done (cf. Luke 10:13-16).

All this "fantastic" picture of the fate of God's enemies may well be expressed in equally fantastic terms for our day. As someone has put it, "Hell can be described as a state of eternal obsession with guilt so that one is actually unable to accept forgiveness. The flames of hell are then the rejected flames of God's love." The reality of God's judgment is too often side-tracked today by a generation that is squeamish about taking the concept of hell seriously. Yet the Song does not end here. The next verse "fulfills" this picture of total judgment. Evidently it is placed here to demonstrate that God's total redeeming grace is commensurate with his wrath.

However, we might ask the very deep question, is hell eternal? The answer, derived from this our "quarry," is Yes and No. It deserves to be eternal, but since God is *in* his chosen ones in hell, so grace abounds.

> v. 43 Praise, O heavens, his people,
>   worship him, all you gods!
>   For he will avenge the blood of his children,
>   and take vengeance on his adversaries;
>   he will repay those who hate him,
>   and cleanse the land for his people.

The first line of this verse presents us with difficulties. First, its grammar is questionable. The Hebrew reads "Rejoice (not NRSV 'praise'), O you nations, his people." Second, the LXX adds a line: "Rejoice ye heavens with him (his people) *and let all the nations of God worship him.*" Hebrews 1:6 seems to quote this extra line from the Greek, since it is not in the original Hebrew, yet at Rom. 15:10 Paul quotes what could be an interpretation of the first Hebrew line. The Epistle to the Hebrews, however, is evidently working upon an amalgam of seven OT quotations. On the other hand, if we understand the Hebrew of Deut. 32:43 as it is, we are able to get good sense: "Rejoice, O you nations, (all of whom are) his people." In parallel with that line the LXX invites all the "angels" to worship God — all

God's "living" creation, all human beings below, all heavenly beings above, as one. Why should they do so? For the wonders of God's handiwork in bringing into being the sun, moon, and stars? No, "for he will avenge the blood of his children" — that is, God completes the redemption of his servant people, Israel (as at v. 35). For the variant readings in the Dead Sea Scrolls of this verse, see Patrick Skehan, "A Fragment of the 'Song of Moses' (Deut. 32) from Qumran."

The people whom God had led out of Egypt as a rabble of slaves God had brought into a special relationship with himself through the imposition of the Covenant (Exod. 19:5-6). By this means God had forged these slaves into what he himself had called them, "his people." God's people then were to be holy, even as God is holy, to use a phrase that occurs again and again in the Holiness Code (Lev. 17–26). To be holy, even as God is holy, therefore reveals the meaning of the second item in God's own choice of revelatory language. God's holiness is the holiness of love, care, compassion, and self-giving, so that Israel in their turn is to approach the nations in that spirit as a "kingdom of priests," as God's servant people to the masses of humanity. Israel had been chosen to mediate the love of God to the peoples of the earth. Moreover, just as priests who handle the sacrifices must be pure and holy in their own lives, if they are to reveal in their capacity as God's servant people the sacrificial love forever present in the heart of God, so too must their angelic counterparts be pure and holy.

The subtitle we have given to this study of the Song of Moses is *A Theological Quarry*. Accordingly, from this verse Deutero-Isaiah, living in the painful period of the Exile, discovered why God had led "his people," his "servant people," to be confronted with the misery of life in Babylonia. The prophet saw that Israel in exile was to be "a light to the nations, that my salvation (embodied in their very persons) may reach to the end of the earth." They were in fact to be "my servant, Israel, in whom I will be glorified" (Isa. 49:3, 6). God was teaching Israel this truth existentially by "sending" his people as his servant to a gentile land, Babylon.

The fate of the nations thus depended utterly upon God's revelation of himself in and through his relationship to his people Israel. Yet Israel was a sinful and disloyal nation: only God could redeem such a situation. God alone could "avenge the blood of his servants" (RSV) and render them to be the chosen instrument of his redemptive purpose. For there is no redemption without the shedding of blood. We shall therefore return to this mystery presently. Without God's first acting thus in Israel there could be no salvation for the Gentiles. And the reality is that God does so act in his prevenient grace. No wonder, then, Moses, in both hope and faith, could call upon "you nations" to "rejoice," or, closer to the Hebrew, to "raise a grand shout of joy" (the hiphil of the verb *ranan*). This meaning of the verb is found at Job 38:7, where *ranan* is paralleled with *yari'ou:* "when the morning stars sang together and all the sons of God shouted for joy" (MT). No wonder Moses' Song reaches its climax here at Deut. 32:43, as an invitation to an exuberant song of joy.

Incidentally, at Matt. 5:43-44 we have the words of Jesus: "You have heard that it was said, 'You shall love your neighbor and hate your enemy.' But I say to you, Love your enemies." The Dead Sea Scrolls Manual of Discipline was circulating in Jesus' day. It is unlikely that our village carpenter learned of it in the local synagogal school. Yet he may have been informed of the Scrolls' existence and learned of their main thrust from such sympathetic Pharisees as Nicodemus, with whom he may well have conversed. In the Manual of Discipline we read, "Love all the children of light . . . and hate all the children of darkness," words to which Jesus probably referred. On the other hand, Jesus himself was then actually "fulfilling" Deut. 32:43, this climax to the Song of Moses.

Mária Eszenyei Széles, commenting on Zeph. 3:9-13, describes the mighty and ultimate "change" that takes place in God's heart when he executes his justice in such a manner that he does not bring about annihilation upon faithless Israel, his thankless children, but instead takes the weight of their rebellion upon himself and bears it himself upon his own heart (*Wrath and Mercy,* 107). Zephaniah has evidently built his theological insight upon this last verse of the Song of Moses, which we now know was uttered some five hundred years before Zephaniah's day. In other words, Moses' Song is nowhere about "religion," nor is it about mankind's search for God. It is about God, the God who reveals his unspeakably great mercy in and through his profound acts of judgment.

According to Exod. 32:30 Moses told the people, "You have sinned a great sin. But now I will go up to the LORD; perhaps I can make atonement for *(kipper be'ad)* your sin." Moses is even ready to die, not for Israel's "sin" but actually for such "sin*ners*" as they had shown themselves to be. But God does not accept his offer. We note two issues here. First, since Moses himself is a sinner, his dying for Israel would not really be expiatory but merely a dramatic act. Second, since Moses as a mere creature *(adam)* of God, created *in the image of God,* offers to make such a total sacrifice, then the fact of his offer reveals that the all-holy and sinless God, his Creator, could and does offer himself as the atonement for his people.

God's act of atonement therefore must be a total sacrificial act. It must "cover" *(kipper)*, first in the human sphere, the whole area of total justice — blood for blood, life for life, wound for wound, stripe for stripe — all that has been caused by that human sin which disrupts the power of the Covenant and fellowship between God and mankind. This it must do in an act of re-creation. The LXX understands this verse to mean "purge" *(ekkathariei)*, in the sense of total, complete, thorough cleansing. Moreover, it grasps also the nuances of the previous verbs in that it employs *ekdikatai* for "avenges" in order to stress the element of judgment in the cleansing. When earlier we considered the significance of the noun *aharit* we noted how the eschatological reverse of judgment is actually mercy. Such is also the case in the LXX reading *antapodosei diken*, meaning "gives back justice to his enemies" (cf. Deut. 32:41).

Now God's act of atonement, being total, must take into account the physical element in mankind. So we return to the crucial concept of blood. So holy is blood, mankind's "life-fluid," that when it is poured on the ground in an act of destructive wickedness it "contaminates" the very soil (Gen. 3:17-19; 4:11-12) or, to express this belief in modern terms, it affects mankind's natural environment. Mankind is not saved "out of" this wicked world. Mankind is saved along with and as part of God's splendid but fallen creation (cf. Rom. 8:18-24a). Thus Moses is not concerned with the salvation of individual souls, but with the establishment of the kingdom of God, as the church father Cyprian (died A.D. 258) noted. Then Israel, restored by the power of God's redemptive love, will once again be known as 'am elohim, the people of God (see Walter Brueggemann, *The Land*). This will come about through the *obverse* divine power of the shedding of blood by sinful mankind.

As a fact of history Israel has never died out. Despite seeming annihilation under Nebuchadnezzar God brought a remnant back to Zion. So it is idle to say today that the Church will die and disappear, because God's grace will always call upon his people to be the servant of the world. Therefore we must reject the theology of Rudolf Bultmann, and that of many modern scholars, who presuppose that the OT and the NT offer us two different religions.

At this point we should turn back to the chapter of Deuteronomy which precedes our Song. The verses at Deut. 31:26-29 comprise a speech by Moses addressed to 'ammo ("his people"), God's chosen people. Of course this setting of the Song was composed in that later century when the book of Deuteronomy found its final shape; but we must remember that this context was shaped on the basis of the original Song. Moses concludes at 31:29, "For *I* (very strong Hebrew expression) know that after my death you will surely act corruptly. . . . In time to come trouble will befall you, because you will do what is evil in the sight of the LORD, provoking him to anger. . . ." Then Moses "recited the words of this Song . . . in the hearing of the whole assembly of Israel" (v. 30).

We may now put together as one whole our translation of each of the sections of v. 43 as discussed above. We have been critical of the NRSV rendering on the ground that it relies more upon the Greek of the LXX than on the MT. Although there may indeed be textual corruptions in the Hebrew, it is our duty to keep as close as possible to the text at hand. So the verse may read:

> Raise a shout of joy you (gentile) nations,
>   (all of whom are) his people,
>   (Be sure that) he will make expiation for the blood
>   of his servants, and will repay his enemies
>   (the Israelites) with *shalom* (see v. 35).
> He will atone both for his people and
>   for their environment.

We have now seen in the words of the Song just how Israel did indeed provoke God to anger, and just "what trouble will befall you." We are to recognize that the degree of wrath such as can be God's alone must necessarily be displayed toward Israel. But now suddenly, and to sum up the whole Song, we hear something very different — "raise a shout of joy!" — a call made to all the peoples of the earth. We do not hear, "*Weep and lament in fear and horror*, for God avenges the blood of his servants."

As noted before, the prophet Isaiah hews aspects of his proclamation from here. He declares that while Yahweh makes use of a pagan nation to chastise and educate his covenant people, that particular pagan nation must inevitably pay the price of their lust for blood and booty (cf. Isa. 10:5-11). The words "his adversaries" in the second line of Deut. 32:43 can mean either "Israel's adversaries" or "God's adversaries." Most likely it means both at once, for Israel itself in its folly was as much God's adversary as were the Amalekites or the Canaanites.

We must keep in mind also the belief in the absolute holiness of blood in the theology of all OT writers. God's covenant with Israel had been sealed by "the blood of the covenant" (Exod. 24:8; cf. Mark 14:24), the emphasis in both Testaments being upon the absolute holiness of blood (cf. 1 Cor. 11:25). Surely then this verse means that God "avenges," for God *must* avenge if he is to remain true to his nature as Rock, in the manner described at Deut. 32:41. God must take the heinousness of Israel's apostasy upon his own heart, since God is united with Israel in a blood-covenant relationship, if he is to set Israel free from its guilt. The judgment can be neither minimized nor abolished. And so we find we must return to what Moses has already said at vv. 35 and 41. God's vengeance upon Israel will be to requite (*shillem*) his people, with *shalom* (cf. Luke 18:8; Rev. 6:10). In fact, so basic to revelation is Deut. 32:43 that it is quoted seven times in the NT. At the same time no other interpretation of v. 43 is possible if both Israel and the nations are not to shrink back in horror when they are summoned to shout for joy. This is what vengeance means for God. God accepts the judgment made upon all humanity, taking it upon himself, and then he sets his people free. In other words the OT describes God as suffering because of people's rejection (cf. Ps. 78:40; Jer. 48:35-36). God has "internalized the people's rejection" (Terence E. Fretheim, *The Suffering of God*, 143). Moses makes it clear therefore that suffering belongs to the person and purpose of God, and his Song forms a revelatory link to the NT and the theology of the Cross.

So it is that "Once we have come to terms with the limitations which language can impose upon thought, we better appreciate those embarrassing passages [e.g., Deut. 32:43b!] which appear on the surface to be gloat songs over a fallen enemy, but which are intended as psalms of thanksgiving that divine justice does not for ever allow tyranny to prosper" (G. B. Caird, *The Language and Imagery of the Bible*, 13; Erhard S. Gerstenberger, "Enemies in the Psalms").

We learn from this passage also that there is no call upon Israel to repent *before* God can or is willing to "make expiation" for his people. Rather, God has compassion on his servants "when they are at their lowest ebb" (v. 36). God acts first to rescue his people even before they repent and return (*shub*) to him — a favorite verb of the prophets. We find here that we are in the same thought world as that of Paul when he declared, "While we still were sinners Christ died for us" (Rom. 5:8), and of the Church catholic down the ages, in that it demonstrates the "prevenient grace" of God in baptizing infants who thus receive the Holy Spirit before they can even ask for it.

Moses, as we have seen, knows that God is a God of action, in that he is the "living" God unlike the Baals and Ashtoreth of Israel's neighbors. God "interferes" in mankind's predicament. Thus this God of all-holiness and of all-love decided, in the beginning of Israel's story, to enter history and to *make* a decisive *act* of expiation. Such an act would be God's chosen means of atonement ("at-one-ment") when God would *shillem*, that is, equalize Israel's shame with an act equaling it in sacrificial love. In that act God's holiness, righteousness, truth, reliability (rocklikeness), grace, mercy, forbearance, and compassion would be finally revealed, including God's re-creative purpose spoken of in Deut. 32:39. This ultimate act of expiation would then reveal that God uses evil to bring forth good, love out of apathy, life out of death.

We are left with two Hebrew words to examine, "(his) land" (*adimato*) and "his people" (*ammo*). Right away we must be aware that "his land" is not the "land" of Israel. That would require the noun *erets,* the word used three times already in our Song. Instead we are to note that *adamah* is a feminine noun, corresponding to the masculine *adam*. At Gen. 2:7, a passage very much older than the "theological" description of creation in Gen. 1, we have "the Lord GOD formed *adam* from the dust of the *adamah*." This choice of terms suggests that *adam* ("man and woman") is of the earth, earthy, and was created by God in close relationship to all the rest of creation — in fact, emphasizing that all creation is one. We are always to keep in mind that the Hebrews were the only Near Eastern people (from Mesopotamia in the east and north to Egypt in the south, from Greece and its colonies in the "west" to the Indus Valley and its very different "Indic" culture in the east) who never, ever thought in dualistic categories. For Moses therefore heaven and earth are one (see above at Deut. 32:8), matter and spirit are one, life here and hereafter are one, body and soul are one, sex and love are one, this world and eternity are one — all because God is one and God's creation is one (Eph. 4:4-6). The only divisive element is the fact of sin, which separates God from mankind and human from human. This is a concept virtually unknown to the "Gentiles" and to the Greek philosophers, whose word Western civilization idolizes. There is thus in OT thought no such thing as the salvation of the "soul" apart from the body. Moreover, there is no resurrection of the soul without that of the body too.

If God then is going to "make expiation" for "his people," as his spiritual sons and daughters, he must necessarily make expiation for their physical framework, their ecological setting, their environment, their human situation. So we must emphasize that this verse makes no reference to the land of Palestine as such, but should be seen in the light of the deliberate relatedness of mankind to their environment revealed to us by the biblical writers' deliberate juxtaposition of the words *adam* and its feminine *adamah* in the "Priestly" account of the creation. *Adamah*, in other words, is indeed part of and one with *adam*, in that for mankind she is "Mother Earth."

Are we then to do with our two Hebrew words what all the Versions do, seek to make sense of them by paraphrasing them or by altering the text? The RSV does so in translating by "the land of his people," following the Greek and Latin Versions. But as we have shown, "his people" and "their environment" together form one entity. The greatness of God is that he is the Savior, not merely of a person's "soul" but of the whole of the complex and wonderful creation of which humanity is but a part. This is a reality that is fully proclaimed in the NT. Consequently there is no need for us to mutilate the Hebrew text.

In *The Future of Creation* Jürgen Moltmann writes, "Gen. 1:28 will have to be interpreted in an entirely new way. We should not read, 'God said to *adam*, Be fruitful and multiply, and fill the earth and "regulate" it,' but 'free it through fellowship with it' " (129-30), as a result of God's "expiation" mentioned in Deut. 32:43. "We shall not be able to achieve social justice,"

Moltmann continues, "without justice to the natural environment." Claus Westermann affirms, "Something like *creatio continua* is what we find in the OT, since both creation and redemption are of grace, and so both are revelatory" (a continuing theme in Westermann and Friedemann Golka, *What Does the OT Say about God?*). In fact we might conclude by recognizing, with James A. Carpenter, that nothing happens apart from grace (*Nature and Grace*, 166). God's grace is his loving, creative approach to the whole of his creation.

God's grace alone, then, re-creates the people of God to be God's instrument as his kingdom of priests to all mankind. Despite the reality that they continue to be sinners, they are now destined to *be* God's light and his salvation to the end of the earth (Isa. 49:6). No wonder when they learn of this all nations, the heavens, and even inanimate nature will shout for joy (Isa. 44:23; Rev. 5:13). They will have learned from Israel that they too have been claimed by Israel's God to be his children and to serve God as his instruments for the redemption of the world.

Postscript

No line can be drawn to separate the theology of the Song of Moses and the theology of the NT, summed up as it is in what Rev. 15:3 calls the Song of the Lamb. We remember that the NT names the OT "the Scriptures," and declares that "all scripture is inspired by God and is useful for teaching, for reproof, for correction, and for training in righteousness" (2 Tim. 3:16). The early Church possessed the OT alone as its Scriptures for its first fifty years. Consequently Christian orthodoxy was thought through, set forth, and proclaimed — even before the rise of the church fathers — and was understood only from the utterances of "Moses and all the prophets." Jesus himself was the source of this belief. He said, "If you believed Moses, you would believe me, for he wrote about me. But if you do not believe what he wrote, how will you believe what I say?" (John 5:46-47).

Throughout the centuries there have been many deviations from this Christian orthodoxy. Today there are pseudo-churches and strange cults galore, all centering on the person of Christ. These all claim to offer people the salvation of their souls. Even within the mainline churches there are those who deviate from the truth enshrined in the Song of the Lamb. In every single case this has come about through rejection of the OT, and so of the contents of the Song of Moses — most often by those who see no need to "put the OT back into the Bible."

This is totally regrettable in that Jesus, as a true Israelite and a son of the Covenant, was Israel's "second chance" to be the servant and the son of the all-holy God. With no awareness of how God handled Israel's first chance, modern deviationists are therefore unable to understand how God the Rock, in his unfailing faithfulness, has handled the life and death and resurrection of Jesus the Christ. Their chief interest is how to save their own souls rather than to make disciples of all nations. In doing this they lose the basic emphasis in Jesus' teaching: "If any want to become my followers, let them deny themselves (the pursuit of their own salvation) and take up their cross daily and follow me. For those who want to save their *psyche* ('soul') will lose it . . ." (Luke 9:23-24). For those who have never read or been instructed in the OT, the Jesus of the Gospels is as little understood as the prophet Mohammed. Jesus then "is seen only as a soft, gentle, unresisting, meek and humble figure, as he was in Pietism, or in nineteenth and twentieth-century Catholicism (the sacred heart!): a feeble image of Jesus" (Hans Küng, *Christianity and the World Religions*, 117). See above at Deut. 32:22.

The word "Lamb" summons up before our eyes the whole realm of sacrifice with which the book of Leviticus is concerned, and what the Song of Moses declares belongs in the very heart of God. Moses then is more than a prophet. He is the instrument God elected to reveal his plan of the redemption of all creation, eventually through the cross of Christ. And the Song of Moses is the exciting, creative summary of God's revelation of his very self — in God's own words!

That is why Emil Brunner could write even in 1934 in the face of the Nazi threat to the Church: "The Church stands or falls with the OT, as it likewise stands or falls with Jesus Christ. Without the OT there is no Jesus Christ. The OT is related to the NT as is the beginning of a sentence to the end. Only the whole sentence, with beginning and end, gives the sense" (*Die Unentbehrlichkeit des Alten Testaments*, 26). With the rediscovery of the OT as Holy Scripture within the last generation, at long last many theological seminaries and colleges are returning to the study of even a little Hebrew, along with detailed study not just of "OT Introduction" or "The History of Israel," but of the central issue of "OT Theology."

To summarize, we have noted that the Song of Moses deals first with the very nature of God and with God's faithfulness to his people. This faithfulness never changes so that it is present through the Covenant made with God's elected people, and will remain so into all eternity.

We learned at Deut. 32:4 that God's work is "perfect." God is the Creator (v. 6), and he has continued to create ever since he began to do so (Gen. 1:1). Moses declares this with confidence and certainty, even in a world of earthquakes, famines, and human wickedness. He does so since he believes this world is God's *good* creation (Gen. 1:31). Jesus agrees with Moses when with magnificent certainty he teaches us to pray, "Your kingdom come . . . on earth *as it is in heaven.*" It is in heaven, the ultimate *shalom* of God (Deut. 32:4), that all things will have reached their "fullness" in God. Yet this *shalom,* understandably at the back of the coin, will be reached only because it is in this world now that humanity's salvation occurs (cf. Hans Küng, *Eternal Life?*). This means again that we cannot overlook the seriousness of history, for each moment in time is unique and unrepeatable, even as is our human experience of it.

We noted in the text that Moses shows no belief in a personal survival of death. But Moses' concern is not for himself or his fellow human beings. His concern is that the Rock remains the Rock "into" eternity. Moses' use of the term "Rock" pictorializes the faithfulness of God. God has made a covenant with his people that will remain forever, for God remains forever. Consequently dying and death, judgment, heaven and hell are all aspects of God's unshakable, rocklike faithfulness. It is this argument that Jesus uses: "Have you not read what was said to you by God, 'I am (not 'was') the God of Abraham, the God of Isaac, and the God of Jacob'? He is God not of the dead, but of the living" (Matt. 22:32).

Because it is an exposition of the Sinai covenant, the Song

deals with the relationship between matter and spirit, heaven and earth, body and soul, mankind and nature. In consequence the Song shows awareness that God's creative and saving love extends to the whole of his creation ("God so loved the *world* . . .").

The Song reveals that God's love for sinners is such that he bears upon his own heart "the iniquity of us all," so that "upon him was the punishment that made us whole" (*sh-l-m*, Isa. 53:5b, 6c). Then we find that God is not just good, but is good *for*; God is there *for* his chosen people. Such is the extent of God's humility and unassuming loving presence. God humbly grants his people complete free will, to the extent that they may reject and even deny him. Thus God's might and power as Creator are revealed in a manner no sinful human could have invented. God will not force his creatures to obey him, but may actually hide his face from them in despair. Thus as humanity's Creator God creates mankind anew by *loving sinners*, for through the grace of forgiveness God lets love create love, not hate.

Moses shows therefore that God wins over his creation by bearing on his own heart the pain of their rejection of him. The NT thus has at hand a theology of the cross of Christ that has been *there* since the beginning of creation. As Jürgen Moltmann puts it, "The Christian hope lies in the *crucified* Son of Man. That is where the wholly other kingdom of God has set foot on earth, fulfilling the revelation of the pain in the heart of God" (*Man*, 2:44).

The greatness and majesty of God's forgiving love that makes his people "whole" is the obverse of the greatness of God's detestation, not of sin but of sinners. God's judgment upon even his own chosen people must necessarily be in terms of "an eye for an eye, a life for a life." The grace God reveals in his total rehabilitation of his people into a *shalom* that is eschatologically significant for all eternity must therefore be commensurate with God's total judgment upon them (cf. Rom. 11:32).

The Song of Moses is explicitly a "teaching" (Deut. 32:2)

from God himself. That is, it is a form of *torah* and is therefore "revelation." To begin with, it teaches that God is *one*. Of the three great monotheistic faiths — Judaism, Christianity, and Islam — all are basically totally different from the "manmade" religions of the East — Hinduism, Buddhism, Zen, and the rest. They are also quite "other" than the religions or philosophies of biblical times — Baal worship in the Levant, Zoroastrianism in Persia, the "religious philosophies" of Plato and Aristotle, the Stoics and Epicureans, the ancient religious heritage of the Egyptians (see Küng, *Christianity and the World Religions*, 77). Consequently our Song has something very pointed to "teach" us all at the present day.

We are now at the beginning of a new era in the life of the world. Westerners have by and large lost faith in the living God, the loving God, the creating God and have fallen back into interest in the hundred and one superstitions we like to call "the religion of the New Age." Neither Judaism nor Islam as well is immune from this collapse of the human spirit. These superstitions that Moses calls belief in strange ("foreign") gods (Deut. 32:12) or "demons" (v. 17) lead only to the chaos of life he experienced under the pharaohs, the chaos in creation that Jeremiah feared, to which we have referred above. Not only so, but such a reversal of God's plan for the planet earth as belief in these gods entails will produce its own eschatological significance in the beyond. For the here and now and the beyond are like two sides of the one coin. This belief will reveal its destructive power in the realm of the spirit also. This is what the book of Revelation "reveals" to us harshly in picture form.

A significant answer to the present landslide of faith in God would be for Judaism, Christianity, and Islam to set aside any rivalry that they may be exhibiting to a doubting world and in companionship reexamine their common roots in the faith of Moses. After all, the Koran lays great stress on Islam's heritage in both Abraham and Moses. Mohammed learned from Moses' Song to call God "the merciful *(ar-rahman)* and the compassionate *(ar-rahim)*." Judaism of course heralds Moses as the one and only true instrument that God has raised up to lead his people to faith and obedience. It was at the Transfiguration (Luke 9:28-36) that Jesus was assured by God that as the Chosen One, the son of God, he was to lead the ultimate "exodus" (the Greek word at Luke 9:31) from chaos to fulfillment and *shalom* — in the footsteps of Moses! Elijah too was present on that mountaintop — Elijah whose name is greatly revered in the Koran. He had fled to that same Mt. Sinai (or Horeb) to hear from God what his election to service entailed. Centuries later Elijah's flight inspired Mohammed's flight (the Hegira) from Mecca to Medina. It was only at Medina that Mohammed came across the names of Moses and Elijah as well as of Jesus, for it was there that he met with the "people of the Book" (as he, and Muslims to this day, called Jews and Christians). In Medina Mohammed encountered the Song of Moses for the first time.

Later theologians among the prophets went on to clarify and express in terms of their contemporary social setting Moses' own rather compact modes of expression. They copied Moses by uttering their message (as did he) in the language of poetry. These prophets continued to declare that the all-holy God, who had so long before revealed himself to Moses at the bush (Exod. 3), was always the same transcendent Judge of all the earth, even while he was also unchangingly the same immanent Savior of both mankind and creation.

Moses' choice of the name "Rock" for God is thus basic to all else that we learn about the LORD and his redemptive purpose, plan, and presence. The name rock tells us that God's *hesed* (his "steadfast love") remains the same forever, even in and through his loathing of evil and the necessary administration of his justice. It also tells us that God is ever the same "Redemptive Lover" of his chosen people, never ceasing to bear the pain and suffering they cause him in his own heart. Finally, as Immanuel, immanent in the servant and from within the ancient (Gk. *palaios*) covenant, God conferred upon his covenant people once and for all his New "Reconstituted" Covenant in the *blood* and *sacrifice* of Jesus Christ.

This does not mean that God had no more to do with his ancient covenant people once the New Covenant was established. As we have reiterated, God is the Rock and so does not change, but remains loyal to his word and promise. Yet just because he is God of the three monotheistic faiths that share the promise about "the land" (or the "earth" or indeed "matter," Deut. 32:43), the Song of Moses could still become the catalyst to bring Judaism, Christianity, and Islam into a closer relationship in the one Abrahamic (or Mosaic) faith. The Song affords us *revelation* of the nature as well as the creative and redemptive purpose of God. It speaks of God's plan for his creation in terms of the election of a servant who is to be his instrument in the redemption of the land. It speaks of love for that uncouth and rebellious servant, of love that goes unspeakably deep for one who is both ugly and unlovable, producing in the Lover himself pain beyond all human understanding.

The Song speaks of a Lover who patiently waits until the servant finally discovers that he cannot raise himself from "hell" by his own bootstraps but must wait in total dependence upon the grace of God. This grace is revealed *at that point* of total abnegation when, as recognition of his Rock-like being, God wholly "vindicates" his chosen servant, granting him absolution and fullness of life *(shalom)* in fellowship with himself — healing out of brokenness, life out of death. Since mortal mankind is one with its environment, the healing reaches even to the created universe. That is how God makes both the universe and humanity into a new creation.

What we have revealed to us through the Word uttered in this humanly conceived poem is a picture of total judgment, absolute love, mercy, and forgiveness — complete *shalom.* It was necessary for a Deutero-Isaiah to show us later that this good news of the whole re-creation — both of God's world and of God's chosen people — is to be passed on to all mankind by this people whom God has first rescued and restored. God does so through the strength of the love and grace that he first bestows upon this people of his choice. Thereby God enabled *them* to *be* his salvation "to the end of the earth" (Isa. 49:6 MT). God does so finally in the One whom on the Mount of Trans-figuration God declared was to complete the "exodus" of the creation from death to life.

Selected Bibliography

Books Cited

Blanch, Stuart.
For All Mankind: A New Approach to the Old Testament (London: Bible Reading Fellowship and John Murray, 1977).

Bonhoeffer, Dietrich.
Letters and Papers from Prison, ed. Eberhard Bethge, 2nd ed. (London: SCM, 1971).

Brown, Raymond E.
The Critical Meaning of the Bible (New York: Paulist, 1981).

———.
The Gospel According to John I-XII. Anchor Bible (Garden City: Doubleday, 1966).

Brueggemann, Walter.
The Land. Overtures to Biblical Theology (Philadelphia: Fortress, 1977).

———.
To Pluck Up, To Tear Down: A Commentary on the Book of Jeremiah 1-25. International Theological Commentary (Grand Rapids: Wm. B. Eerdmans and Edinburgh: Handsel, 1988).

147

Brunner, Emil.
Die Unentbehrlichkeit des Alten Testaments für die mission-ierende Kirche (Stuttgart: Evang. Missionsverlag, 1934).

Caird, George B.
The Language and Imagery of the Bible (Philadelphia: West-minster and London: Duckworth, 1980).

Carpenter, James A.
Nature and Grace: Toward an Integrated Perspective (New York: Crossroad, 1988).

Cornill, Carl Heinrich.
Introduction to the Canonical Books of the Old Testament (London: Williams & Norgate and New York: Putnam's, 1907).

Craigie, Peter C.
The Book of Deuteronomy. New International Commentary on the Old Testament (Grand Rapids: Wm. B. Eerdmans, 1976).

Driver, Samuel Rolles.
A Critical and Exegetical Commentary on Deuteronomy. International Critical Commentary (Edinburgh: T. & T. Clark and New York: Scribner's, 1895).

Eichrodt, Walter.
Theology of the Old Testament, vol. 2. Old Testament Library (Philadelphia: Westminster and London: SCM, 1967).

Fretheim, Terence E.
The Suffering of God: An Old Testament Perspective. Over-tures to Biblical Theology (Philadelphia: Fortress, 1984).

Frye, Northrop.
Words with Power: Being a Second Study of the Bible and Literature (San Diego: Harcourt Brace Jovanovich, 1990).

Gowan, Donald E.
From Eden to Babel: A Commentary on the Book of Genesis 1-11. International Theological Commentary (Grand Rapids: Wm. B. Eerdmans and Edinburgh: Handsel, 1988).

Gray, John.

The Legacy of Canaan, 2nd ed. Supplements to Vetus Testamentum 5 (1965).

Hengel, Martin.

Jews, Greeks and Barbarians: Aspects of the Hellenization of Judaism in the Pre-Christian Period (Philadelphia: Fortress, 1980).

Heschel, Abraham J.

The Prophets (New York: Harper & Row and Jewish Publication Society of America, 1962).

Huart, Clement I.

A History of Arabic Literature (London: W. Heinemann and New York: D. Appleton, 1903).

Jeremias, Jörg.

Die Reue Gottes: Aspekte alttestamentlicher Gottesvorstellung. Biblische Studien 65 (Neukirchen-Vluyn: Neukirchener Verlag, 1975).

Jüngel, Eberhard.

The Doctrine of the Trinity: God's Being Is in Becoming (Grand Rapids: Wm. B. Eerdmans and Edinburgh: Handsel, 1976).

Kitamori, Kazoh.

Theology and the Pain of God, 5th ed. (Richmond: John Knox and London: SCM, 1966).

Knight, George A. F.

The New Israel: A Commentary on the Book of Isaiah 56-66. International Theological Commentary (Grand Rapids: Wm. B. Eerdmans and Edinburgh: Handsel, 1985).

————.

Servant Theology: A Commentary on the Book of Isaiah 40-55. International Theological Commentary (Grand Rapids: Wm B. Eerdmans and Edinburgh: Handsel, 1984).

————, **and Golka, Friedemann W.**

Revelation of God: A Commentary on the Books of the Song of Songs and Jonah. International Theological Commentary

(Grand Rapids: Wm. B. Eerdmans and Edinburgh: Handsel, 1988).

Küng, Hans.
Christianity and the World Religions (Garden City: Doubleday, 1986).

──────.
Eternal Life? Life after Death as a Medical, Philosophical, and Theological Problem (Garden City: Doubleday, 1984).

Lapide, Pinchas, and Moltmann, Jürgen.
Jewish Monotheism and Christian Trinitarian Doctrine (Philadelphia: Fortress, 1979).

Martin-Achard, Robert, and Re'emi, S. Paul.
God's People in Crisis: A Commentary on the Books of Amos and Lamentations. International Theological Commentary (Grand Rapids Wm. B. Eerdmans and Edinburgh: Handsel, 1984).

Metz, Johannes Baptist.
Theology of the World (New York: Herder & Herder and Tunbridge Wells: Burns & Oates, 1969).

Moltmann, Jürgen.
The Crucified God (New York: Harper & Row and London: SCM, 1974).

──────.
The Future of Creation (Philadelphia: Fortress and London: SCM, 1979).

──────.
Man: Christian Anthropology in the Conflicts of the Present (Philadelphia: Fortress and London: SCM, 1971).

Nicoll, W. Robertson.
Princes of the Church (London: Hodder & Stoughton, 1921).

Oden, Thomas C.
The Living God: Systematic Theology, Volume I (San Francisco: Harper & Row, 1987).

von Rad, Gerhard.
Deuteronomy. Old Testament Library (Philadelphia: Westminster and London: SCM, 1966).

———.

Old Testament Theology, 2 vols. (New York: Harper & Row and Edinburgh: Oliver & Boyd, 1962, 1965).

Rahner, Karl.

The Practice of Faith (London: SCM, 1982 and New York: Crossroad, 1983).

Richardson, Alan.

Christian Apologetics (New York: Harper and London: SCM, 1948).

Seale, Morris S.

The Desert Bible: Nomadic Tribal Culture and Old Testament Interpretation (New York: St. Martin's and London: Weidenfeld and Nicolson, 1974).

Smith, Morton.

Palestine Parties and Politics that Shaped the Old Testament (New York: Columbia University Press, 1971).

Song, Choan-Seng.

The Compassionate God (Maryknoll, N.Y.: Orbis and London: SCM, 1982).

Széles, Mária Eszenyei.

Wrath and Mercy: A Commentary on the Books of Habakkuk and Zephaniah. International Theological Commentary (Grand Rapids: Wm. B. Eerdmans and Edinburgh: Handsel, 1987).

Torrance, Thomas F.

The Apocalypse Today (Grand Rapids: Wm. B. Eerdmans and London: James Clark, 1960).

Trible, Phyllis.

God and the Rhetoric of Sexuality. Overtures to Biblical Theology (Philadelphia: Fortress, 1978).

de Vaux, Roland.

The Early History of Israel (Philadelphia: Westminster and London: Darton, Longman & Todd, 1978).

Van Buren, Paul M.

A Christian Theology of the People Israel, 2: *A Theology of the Jewish-Christian Reality* (San Francisco: Harper & Row, 1983).

Vriezen, Theodorus Christiaan.
An Outline of Old Testament Theology, 2nd ed. (Newton Centre, Mass.: Branden and Wageningen: Veenman, 1970).

Walters (Katz), Peter.
The Text of the Septuagint: Its Corruptions and Their Emendations (London: Cambridge University Press, 1973).

Westermann, Claus, and Golka, Friedemann.
What Does the Old Testament Say about God? (Atlanta: John Knox, 1979).

Whale, John S.
Victor and Victim: The Christian Doctrine of Redemption (Cambridge: Cambridge University Press, 1960).

Wolff, Hans Walter.
Anthropology of the Old Testament (Philadelphia: Fortress and London: SCM, 1974).

Wright, George Ernest.
The Old Testament and Theology (New York: Harper and Row, 1969).

Articles

Albright, William Foxwell.
"Some Remarks on the Song of Moses in Deuteronomy xxxii," *Vetus Testamentum* 9 (1959): 339-46.

Davies, G. Henton.
"Deuteronomy," in *Peake's Commentary on the Bible* (New York and London: Nelson, 1962), 269-84.

Gerstenberger, Erhard S.
"Enemies in the Psalms: A Challenge to Christian Preaching." *Horizons in Biblical Theology* 4 (1982): 61-73.

Knight, George A. F.
"Is 'Righteous' Right? *Scottish Journal of Theology,* 41 (1988): 1-10.

———.

"Theophany," in *The International Standard Bible Encyclopedia*, ed. Geoffrey W. Bromiley (Grand Rapids: Wm. B. Eerdmans, 1988), 4:827-31.

Roberts, J. J. M.

"The Davidic Origin of the Zion Tradition," *Journal of Biblical Literature* 92 (1973): 329-44.

Skehan, Patrick W.

"A Fragment of the 'Song of Moses' (Deut. 32) from Qumran," *Bulletin of the American Schools of Oriental Research* 136 (1954): 12-15.

Wright, George Ernest.

"The Lawsuit of God: A Form-Critical Study of Deut. 32," in *Israel's Prophetic Heritage,* ed. Bernhard W. Anderson and Walter Harrelson (New York: Harper and London: SCM, 1962), 26-67.

Other Works

Albright, William Foxwell.

Yahweh and the Gods of Canaan (Garden City: Doubleday and London: Athlone, 1968; repr. Winona Lake: Eisenbrauns, 1978).

Alter, Robert.

The Art of Biblical Poetry (New York: Basic Books and London: Allen & Unwin, 1985).

Baumgärtel, Friedrich.

"The Hermeneutical Problem of the Old Testament," in *Essays on Old Testament Hermeneutics,* ed. Claus Westermann (Atlanta: John Knox, 1979; *Essays on Old Testament Interpretation,* London: SCM, 1963), 134-59.

Blauw, Johannes.

The Missionary Nature of the Church: A Survey of the Biblical Theology of Mission (Grand Rapids: Wm. B. Eerdmans and Cambridge: Lutterworth, 1962).

Bright, John.
Covenant and Promise: The Prophetic Understanding of the Future in Pre-Exilic Israel (Philadelphia: Westminster, 1976).

Brueggemann, Walter.
"A Shape for Old Testament Theology, II: Embrace of Pain." *Catholic Biblical Quarterly* 47 (1985): 395-415.

Childs, Brevard S.
Introduction to the Old Testament as Scripture (Philadelphia: Fortress and London: SCM, 1979).

Chilton, Bruce D.
The Glory of Israel: The Theology and Provenience of the Isaiah Targum (Sheffield: JSOT Press, 1982).

Clements, Ronald E.
God's Chosen People: A Theological Interpretation of the Book of Deuteronomy (London: SCM, 1968).

Coats, George W.
Moses: Heroic Man, Man of God (Sheffield: JSOT Press, 1988).

Crenshaw, James L.
A Whirlpool of Torment: Israelite Traditions of God as an Oppressive Presence. Overtures to Biblical Theology (Philadelphia: Fortress, 1984).

Cross, Frank Moore.
Canaanite Myth and Hebrew Epic (Cambridge, Mass.: Harvard University Press, 1973).

————, and Freedman, David Noel.
Studies in Ancient Yahwistic Poetry. SBL Dissertation Series 21 (Missoula: Scholars Press, 1975).

Cunliffe-Jones, Hubert.
Deuteronomy. Torch Bible Commentaries (London: SCM, 1951).

Eissfeldt, Otto.
Das Lied Moses, Deuteronomium 32,1-43 und das Lehrgedicht Asaphs, Psalm 78. Beihefte zur Zeitschrift für die alttestamentliche Wissenschaft 104/5 (1958).

————.

The Old Testament: An Introduction (New York: Harper and Row and Oxford: Blackwell, 1965).

Gibson, J. C. L., ed.

Canaanite Myths and Legends, 2nd ed. (Edinburgh: T. & T. Clark, 1978).

Gottwald, Norman K.

All the Kingdoms of the Earth (New York: Harper & Row, 1964).

Gowan, Donald E.

When Man Becomes God: Humanism and Hubris in the Old Testament. Pittsburgh Theological Monograph 6 (Pittsburgh: Pickwick, 1975).

Hamlin, E. John.

Inheriting the Land: A Commentary on the Book of Joshua. International Theological Commentary (Grand Rapids: Wm. B. Eerdmans and Edinburgh: Handsel, 1983).

Høgenhaven, Jasper.

Problems and Prospects of Old Testament Theology (Sheffield: JSOT Press, 1988).

Johnstone, William.

"Reactivating the Chronicles Analogy in Pentateuchal Studies," *Zeitschrift für die alttestamentlichen Wissenschaften* 99 (1987): 16-37.

Knibb, Michael A.

"Prophecy and the emergence of the Jewish apocalypses," in *Israel's Prophetic Tradition,* ed. Richard Coggins, Anthony Phillips, and Michael A. Knibb (Cambridge: Cambridge University Press, 1982), 155-180.

Knight, George A. F.

"Israel — the Land and Resurrection," in *The Witness of the Jews to God,* ed. David W. Torrance (Edinburgh: Handsel, 1982), 32-41.

Kutscher, Edward Y.

The Language and Linguistic Background of the Isaiah Scroll (1QIsaᵃ) (Leiden: Brill, 1974).

Moo, Douglas J.
The Old Testament in the Gospel Passion Narratives (Sheffield: Almond, 1983).

Roberts, J. J. M.
"Zion in the Theology of the Davidic-Solomon Empire," in *Studies in the Period of David and Solomon,* ed. Tomoh Ishida (Tokyo: Yamakawa-Suppansha and Winona Lake: Eisenbrauns, 1982), 93-108.

Robertson, David A.
Linguistic Evidence in Dating Early Hebrew Poetry. Society of Biblical Literature Dissertation 3 (Missoula: Scholars Press, 1972).

Robinson, Gnana.
The Origin and Development of the Old Testament Sabbath (Frankfurt: Peter Lang, 1988).

Skehan, Patrick W.
"The Structure of the Song of Moses in Dt. 32, 1-43," *Catholic Biblical Quarterly* 13 (1951): 153-63.

———.
Studies in Israelite Poetry and Wisdom. Catholic Biblical Quarterly Monograph (Washington: Catholic Biblical Association, 1971).

Terrien, Samuel L.
The Elusive Presence: Toward a New Biblical Theology (San Francisco: Harper & Row, 1978).

Weinfeld, Moshe.
Deuteronomy and the Deuteronomic School: The Covenant of the Plains of Moab (Oxford: Clarendon Press, 1972; repr. Winona Lake: Eisenbrauns, 1992).

Welch, Adam C.
Deuteronomy: The Framework of the Code (London: Milford, 1932).

Zimmerli, Walther.
Old Testament Theology in Outline (Atlanta: John Knox and Edinburgh: T. & T. Clark, 1978).

The Song of Moses (Deuteronomy 32) gives an exciting, creative summary of God's self-revelation at Sinai, [...] of God's faithful covenant with his pe[...] biblical scholar and teacher George [...A. F. Kn...] these forty-three verses from one of the most ancient passages in the Bible constitute a quarry out of which much later theology has been hewn.

As Knight shows, theologians from biblical times to our own have developed a theology of remembering from these verses, clarifying and expressing Moses' words in terms of their respective social settings. Originating in God's own words as revealed to Moses, the Song allowed Israel to remember God's mighty acts in history and to summarize those experiences and ideals that would allow them to survive as a people. Beyond that, the Song also sheds important light on Israel's mission-in-covenant to the nations and on that of the Church and Synagogue today.

Written in accord with the aims of the INTERNATIONAL THEOLOGICAL COMMENTARY series, of which Knight serves as coeditor, this volume is for ministers, educators, and students who seek to move beyond the commonly used historical-critical approach to Old Testament interpretation by taking up a theological perspective on the Hebrew text.

GEORGE A. F. KNIGHT is retired as professor and pastor, having served in Hungary, Scotland, New Zealand, the United States, and the Pacific Islands. Coeditor of the INTERNATIONAL THEOLOGICAL COMMENTARY series, he is the author of three ITC volumes — on Isaiah 40–55, on Isaiah 56–66, and on The Song of Songs and Jonah. He has also written the book *I Am: That Is My Name* and commentaries on Leviticus and Psalms in the *Daily Study Bible*.

Cover art: Mt. Sinai ©Art Jacobs
Cover design by Rosemary Ellis

ISBN 0-8028-0599-X

Wm. B. Eerdmans
Publishing Co.
Grand Rapids, Michigan

9 780802 805997